Be Love

Become the Pure Omnibenevolence of The Trinity

Prayers and Scriptures to Own Our Identity in Christ

By LindaJane Chapman via a Holy Spirit Anointing

QR Code to PrayerCoachUSA.com website:

CONTENTS

CONTENTS

CONTENTS

Preface

Dear reader,

This Book is based upon God's Scriptures that made an impact in my life, the mentors who contribute to my growth in Christ salvation and utilizing the gifts of the Holy Spirit which empowered my life. We are in a spiritual battle in every favor and blessing God wants to give us in life, Satan tries to manipulate us away from the blessings by taking us into the vile natures of the flesh. So, as we miss out on God's pure anointing in a moment in time. Through knowing God's word, growing in our spiritual life, we start recognizing our spiritual strengthens and in the natures of the flesh our weaknesses. When we begin to learn to cast out the natures of the flesh is when we learn to be victorious in Christ supernatural authority in us.

Once we learn to utilize God's word, we truly see how easy it is to cast away thoughts of despair and walk in a pure Christlike victorious life. I tell you my true-life stories proving God's word is real in today's world if we choose to use it! The here and now events related to scriptures reveals the power in the word of God. Showing us a reality today that we can exist in right now, not just stories from the Bible characters of long ago who experienced miracles. I have had many miracle interventions from God that changed bad circumstances into good or great circumstances. Now I pray for me to share how the wisdom of God's word blessed my life. I pray a Holy Spirit anointing upon your adventure through these pages. Specific scriptures in a certain order to enlighten you to own your Identity in Christ and walk in the Trinities Omnipresence, Omniscience, Omnipotence, and Omnibenevolence.
The power of being created in God Almighty's image.

THE MENTORS IN MY LIFE:

I have been so very blessed by people who love Christ and have opened their doors for me to share the wisdom of God's word that I personally experienced that truly anointed me in times of serious troubles.

I remember the people I respect who have touched my spirit and helped me overcome my insecurities. Through bible studies they have taught me to have confidence in expressing God's scriptures. Through Christ salvation in me and God's word is how I have learned to be bold in sharing the empowerment of the Holy Spirit anointing. Which conquers Satan's vile natures of the flesh and stops the curse of death Satan birthed into mankind through Adam's disobedience.

My earliest fellowship was with Debbie Boone and Gabriel Ferrer' at a home bible study group in the 70's. Sally Lanivich, the designer, took me to Rosemary Clooney's home in Beverly Hills where Gabreil was teaching a bible study.

The Vineyard church with Kenn Gulliksen introduced me to amazing worship music and a powerful message in scriptures. Pamela Norman aka Pam Newman told me to go there and to the bible studies associated with the church. Al Kasha a two-time academy award winning song writer, He and his wife Ceil had weekly bible studies and Sunday potlucks where we would have water baptisms in their pool.

The Hiding Place with Henry Cutrona; I experienced a true anointing in scriptures, worship, and using the gifts of the spirit in _1st Cor. 12:4-12._ The home fellowship groups gave us a real bonding in Christ. Marty Goetz would come to my home bible study and share his new worship songs he had just written, truly a pure anointing. Later in my life a lyric from a certain song, he wrote truly empowered me in a life and death situation. "He is My defense I will not Be Moved" A Russian Mafia man held a knife to my chin threatening me. "I am going to chop you up in little pieces and no one is going to find you." Later, I will tell this story about how The Trinity protected me!

Hal Lindsey would speak at 6am at Will Rogers Park beach every Sunday and we would learn of the meanings in the book of Revelation.

I learned the true meaning of scriptures in the Hebrew and Greek with Pastor Dale Bergman; teaching us what the scripture meaning meant when it was being lived by the disciples at the time of Jesus.

Learning to memorize scriptures at a private bible study at Dyan Cannon's home truly made a big difference in my confidence and knowledge of how scriptures affect my life. Dyan is very anointed and teaches the importance of memorizing scriptures. Each month she would give us 2 words to find scriptures in the bible, which impressed each of us to memorize and then we would tell what it meant to us personally. Truly, food for thought in learning what and how the scriptures personally touch our life.

"Soldiers for the Second Coming" with Pastor Billy Davis Jr. and Marilyn McCoo, who have an anointed ministry of amazing music, heartfelt prayer requests, plus stories of praise, and thanksgiving. This gave me the ability to overcome my insecurity of speaking God's scriptures in public. I gained confidence when I would get up and share my recent miracle of God's hand in helping me out of difficulties and the blessing's that came from me praising God through my troubles. Also, sharing the anointing that comes from making Godly choices in our life.

Gemma Wenger Ministry gives me back the ability to be in fellowship with mighty Christians to utilize the gifts of the spirit boldly: revelation, speaking in tongues, interpretations of tongues, laying hands on each other in prayer, casting out demons, prophecy, plus worshipping unto the Lord and savior Christ, the word of creation. Also, Gemma interviewed me for one of her TV shows. Plus, she has encouraged me to speak on her Facebook Live broadcasts. I have become composed and have confidence in speaking God's scriptures in sharing my life stories.

Dr Susan Stafford, has inspired many for her care of cancer patients and the work in her ministry as a Chaplin.

 I started praying for people on their death bed and many received Christ as their savior and were not afraid to ascend to heaven after I ministered to them. Their families are always so grateful. I champion each person to boldly speak God's word to people who are battling an illness.

There are many other ministries which I value and have learned from in my life. Salem Family Ministry, Cheryl Salem taught me the "Tones in the Thorne Room" pure worship. In His Presence Church, pastors Mel and Desiree Ayes, teach us to live in spiritual gifts. an inspiring experience.

I always enjoy the message, and worship music with so many friends at Lee Benton Ministries, Int'l plus the truly anointed message each month. Afterwards having dinner at Victorio's restaurant fellowshipping with friends just to name a few, Lee Benton, her husband, David with Terry Moore, Jimmy Espinoza, Cindy Mac, Cynthia Droniak, Mark Weber, and Micheal Krynak is always rewarding.

I share my life experiences to show everyone how God's word is real and very useful in today's world when we choose to use it. We will learn the fullness of HIS power in us for it is perpetually never ending. Lord, I want your gifts to bring wisdom, healing, and God's powers into our lives daily. Enjoy the adventure in your own life.

How we gain spiritual self-control through
owning our identity in Christ

Amen, *Romans 8:28* Praise the Lord in all things. We have two choices in life that have a major effect on our life. When we choose to live by knowing that if we live with a joyful heart, God will give us his power daily even through all the attacks from Satan; by giving us abundant blessings through each of our trials; God guides us in all our endeavors. *Matt. 16:19* We will achieve victory and live in God's kingdom here on earth as it is in heaven. But when we choose to live in negativity over every issue; we live in a battleground of Satan's realm of despair in the natures of the flesh, and Satan will make a bad circumstance worse. Agreeing with Satan's ideas causes illness in our bodies. *Matt. 8:13* Remember each word that we say creates whatever we are saying. Listen to your words and see the results. Stop declaring bad things. Whenever we choose to be negative, we give Satan power over our circumstances. Satan can only work evil if we agree with its ideas. Satan wants us to live in the realm of negativity here on earth. God wants us to live in his playground of abundant joy, creativity, harmony being a light cutting out darkness. Switch on the light changing negative words into positive words. However, we must always use God's wisdom in discernment and perception to guaranty we are not being positive about something that could end up being negative for our life. Be that shining light of victory over evil. *Psalms 32:8,* God Almighty instructs, teaches, and guides us when we listen and obey.

My life experiences reveal what happened when I chose my emotions, making my choices in life verse leaning into my Spirit-being to gain wisdom and power to have victory through my choices in life.

This book of Scriptures to memorize and Prayers are given to defeat any enemy who comes against us. God's word gives us God's kingdom to bless our life's here on earth. Victory is held within our choices in life and how we ask for forgiveness from Christ and/or call out for help from "The Trinity." After we have received Christ salvation redemption, we are to seek to become Christ like: Omnibenevolence is Christ.

By LindaJane Chapman via a Holy Spirit anointing

"BE LOVE"

Become the Pure Omnibenevolence of The Trinity

Prayers and Scriptures to Own Our Identity in Christ

By LindaJane Chapman; via a Holy Spirit anointing.

When you see this *** it means extra important to remember

INTRODUCTION

God gave me these scriptures in a specific order for a certain purpose to excel us in an anointing of HIS word as His children to truly be empowered. When I asked Jesus to show me the depth of HIS Holy Armor through HIS divine word; He led me to these scriptures. Truly bringing a fullness with enhanced knowledge, more understanding held within His scriptures; the powerful meaning of HIS daily armor for us in *Chapter 1 through Chapter 12 Ephesians 6: 10-19.* note: **God's word spoken out loud has power! Read these scriptures' aloud.** *Romans 10:17* . **"Faith comes by hearing and hearing by the word of God." Even if it is only a whisper. It is the spoken word. A moment of silence has NO POWER! It is Satan's goal to silence God's word. We Believers are mighty worthy worker warrior Saints in Christ salvation; it is the scriptures that empower us through The Spirit of Truth.**

A moment of divine thought spoken truly has power. God's word is a living word, so I suggest getting a pad of paper and a pen. When God speaks a certain idea to you through these scriptures write it down immediately. HE is talking to you specifically through HIS words to bless you and your family! Take heed to HIS power in you! Christ is the only way to truly conquer the evil natures of the flesh in mankind. His words are omnipotent, omnipresent, omniscient through you, HIS Saints, when you choose to speak his scriptures. Our goal is to become the Omnibenevolence of the Trinity, " Christlike."

I have had so many supernatural experiences in my life from age eight through last week. God empowers my life when I listen to HIM. When I have not listened for many different reasons; mostly, by Satan fueling the natures of flesh to bamboozle my choices! Yet, when I call on Christ for help; The Lord always gets me through the circumstances: from being shot with a gun, an airplane accident, car accidents, con men in life, three times men physically trying to hurt me and two times trying to kill me. Prayer changed the outcome: to angel visitations, men physically thrown across the room allowing my escape before I would be harmed. Once the amazing delight of light sparks shooting out of my eyes. Strangers bewildered, would remark, "I see light sparks shooting out of your eyes?" I have seen this in four other people in my life, so I was not afraid when it happened to me.

The ugly, the bad and the good to God's great interventions: Several miracle healings, casting fire and storms away from my presence and casting evil out of people trying to hurt me. To amazing blessings of fun stuff that I did: TV shows, Movie Premieres, Music Award shows. The full details of these events are explained in my autobiography. Excerpts of these events are told in align with scriptures in this book. Miracles happen when you own your identity in Christ salvation redemption with the Holy Spirit energy empowerment. I live in it, and you can also when you Trust in God! I recognize Christ omnipresent, omniscient, omnipotent and omnibenevolent power authority moving through me! It is totally in my salvation redemption becoming God's Saint, a warrior here on earth and in heaven. His Scriptures reveal how we as Christians own our identity in being a renewed creation through Christ and the empowerment of the HOLY SPIRIT.

***_John 14:12-28_ "very truly I tell you, whoever believes in me will do the works, I have done, and you will even do greater things than these, because I am going to the Father. And I will do whatever you ask in my name...... I will ask the Father to send the Spirit of Truth {The HOLY SPIRIT} to be with you as an advocate to help you forever!"

***_John 20:21-22_, *"Peace be with you! As the Father, has sent me, I am sending you."* Then *he breathed on them and said, "Receive the Holy Spirit."* _John 14:16-30_ "I will ask the Father, and He will give you another Helper to be with you forever. The helper is The Spirit of Truth. The people of the world cannot accept him or know him. But you know him. He lives in you." We, being renewed in Christ redemption are the temple of the Holy Spirit energy empowerment.

Christ renews each one who receives Him to become saints, recreated in God's image. Do you know who you are? ***_Phil 4:8_ "dwell on whatsoever things is true, just, honest, pure, lovely, a good report" The A+ for what we need to happen in your life. This is not a new-age idea. Satan likes to hijack God's words and create a deviation to stop mankind's power. If you want a truly anointed life, then you must recognize and stop Satan's ideas.

Ask for the anointed ideas in Jesus Name. Allow the thoughts of your mind, passions of your heart, and words within your actions to become great in the HOLY SPIRIT anointing of your life. There are numerous prayers needed so I am giving you, God's scriptures that teach you, who believe in Christ, the empowerment of using His word.

Satan works daily to take Christ's renewed divine power out of humanity. Lucifer aka Satan wanted to be God and Satan wants what we have! Lucifer was not male or female; angels are "its." God purposes certain angels to do certain tasks. Lucifer was the highest Angel in worship and the most beautiful of many angels. Sometimes certain angels (not all angels) can be formed to look like a human being. Yet they do not have the character of a real human being. Lucifer was thrown out of heaven before he knew of this characteristic.

We can now understand clearly why Satan as an "it" has bamboozled people into the woke idea of no male or female. When a human being stops caring about humanity and starts labelling humans as "it, they, them," Satan gets to enslave them into Satan's vile ideas of transforming themselves into no gender beings. Many may desire to become Transgender. One helpless nature of the flesh is in *Romans 7:19-20,* "for I do not do the good I want but do the evil I do not want. If I do that it is no longer me but the sin that dwells within me that, does it." Satan's lusts are put into our flesh to enslaves us!

Christ the word of creation is the only one who can stop spiritual death and conquer the vile natures of the flesh here on earth. God sent Christ to send the Holy Spirit of truth to set us free.

Amen, *Romans 8:28* praise the Lord in all things. We have two choices in life that have a major effect on our life. When we choose to live by knowing that if we live with a joyful heart, God will give us his power daily even through all the attacks from Satan; by giving us abundant blessings in each of our trials God guides us in all our endeavors. We will achieve victory and live in God's kingdom here on earth as it is in heaven. But when we choose to live in negativity over every issue; we live in Satan's realm of despair in the natures of the flesh, and Satan will make a bad circumstance worse. Agreement with Satan's ideas cause illness in our bodies. Remember each word that we say creates whatever we are saying. Listen to your words and see the results. Stop declaring bad things. Whenever we choose to be negative, we give Satan power over our circumstances. Satan can only work evil if we agree with vile ideas. Satan wants us to live in the realm of negativity here on earth. God wants us to live in abundant joy, creativity, harmony in being a light cutting out darkness. Switch on the light changing negative words into positive words. However, we must always use God's wisdom in discernment and perception to guarantee we are not being positive about something that could end up being negative in our life. Be the shining light of victory over evil. *Psalms 32:8* God Almighty instructs, teaches, and guides us when we listen.

My life experiences reveal what happened when I chose my emotions, making my choices in life versus leaning into my spirit-being to gain wisdom and power to gain victory to my choices in life.

Philippians 1:21 we must die to the natures of the flesh to gain the empowerment of Christ's authority in our life. Oh, the messes Christ got me out of because I called on him for help after the fact of first making terrible choices. Make Godly choices and you put yourself in God's playground where Satan cannot enter. Make choices via the natures of the flesh and you will put yourself in Satan's battleground where God comes in to help you have victory over evil. However, you put yourself there by your choices.

This book of scriptures to memorize and prayers are given to defeat any enemy who comes against us. God's word gives us God's kingdom to bless our lives here on earth. Victory is held within our choices in life and how we ask for forgiveness from Christ and/or call out for help from the Trinity. After we have received Christ salvation redemption, we are to seek to become Christlike: Omnibenevolence is Christ

Apostle Lady LindaJane Chapman   PrayerCoachUSA.com

My ministry shows are airing on The CrossTV.com look for

"JesusismyJubileeChurch.org"   Bishop Gerald Jones. LindaJane Chapman Ministry is

" PrayerCoachUSA.com"

Bishop Gerald Jones is giving me the opportunity to be a part of his ministry to share my life stories whereas God's scriptures have saved my life because I learned them and used God's divine word in a time of extreme peril. Live and speak the word of the Lord and gain a changed life of success in stopping Satan from trying to destroy your life.

Bishop Ernest Johnson is giving me a platform on his KTLA Ministry shows, "Jesus Is The Answer" JITA TV, Powerful messages in Christ are shared on his network.

I am very grateful for "Dale Davidson Las Vegas Tonight" my ministry shows that have aired on his network several times and have had requests for reruns. Terry Arnold the Producer is having me come back to talk about my life experiences and my Book "Be Love"

Through Dale Davidson I met Dr Ken Smith of The Marketplace Network and later met Bishop Dominic Contreras. I am an active contributor on their network, Many powerful warrior saints in Christ are featured on TheMarketPlaceNetwork and their eight platforms.

I also broadcast on Vision TV Founded by Adnan Maqsood which reaches the multitudes of households globally

The details of when these shows will air are being placed on my Website " PrayerCoachUSA. com." . If you have any questions, you can reach me via email at HolySpiritOne2@aol.com or PrayerCoachUSA@Yahoo.com

Chapter 1 "We Have a Holy Armor"

This will be an adventure, chapter 1 through "The Prayer of the Morning" in chapter 12, and the scriptures given here **cover many facets of our heavenly power held within our earthly bodies. ***<u>Speaking Scriptures daily empowers our choices.</u>** Reveal your divine path for us, LORD. **2<u>nd</u> _Cor 7:15_** We strive for obedience in our lives through fellowship with you, JESUS. We pray for your abundant blessings Lord for us; including all Christians, Jews, Israelites plus all in our family, friends, and loved ones plus their family, friends and loved ones; while continuing to <u>build Jesus' force of virtue, power and authority</u> across this nation and the world. **Bless us, our redeemer Jesus, "Yahweh", Elohim, Abba, El Shaddai, El Roi, El Elyon, Adonai, Jehovah Rapha, Jehovah Nissi, Jehovah Jireh, and Shalom. These are just a few of the names which describe the powers of "The Lord." Look each one up to see how The Trinity blesses your life.**

Ephesians 6: 10-13 "Finally, my brethren, <u>be strong in the LORD, and the POWER in HIS might.</u> We put on your whole armor Lord that we may be able to stand against the wiles of the devil. For we wrestle not against flesh and blood but against principalities, powers, rulers of darkness of this world and against spiritual wickedness in high places." However, **<u>we are the victor's</u>** as you, Lord, created us in your image and what Adam gave away in Eden was the fall of our true power within you, YHWH(YAH-way). You, Father God, gave your son Jesus, back a divine power for us in the Holy Spirit. We are made higher than the angels and more powerful than Satan and the demons. ** _1st Cor. 6:19-20_ We are the temple of the Holy Spirit. We have Christ resurrection power in us; when we choose to live within that power, instead of allowing the natures of the flesh to rule our life. Remember Satan uses the natures of the flesh to destroy us and others. Evil can only hurt a person when they agree with Satan or do not stop someone who has agreed with Satan's natures of the flesh.**

We command the host of Holy Angels to assist us in all things and rebuke Satan and the 1/3 of the host of fallen angels, (demons) who try to thwart us in all things. (google these scriptures now _1st Timothy 1: 4-17 + 4:1_) **Important note. remember** the fallen angels work through man via Nature's of the Flesh, Psychics,' Mediums', Astrologers etc. Stay away from them. *****_Colossians 2:8 "See to it that no one takes you captive by philosophy, and empty deceit, according to human traditions, according to the elemental demons and evil spirits of the world and 'not according to Christ empowerment of the HOLY SPIRIT'."_** Demons will tell you and the psychic facts about your past, of which to no surprise, "the demons see it," yet the psychic can say what the demon tells them yet the psychic cannot predict the future. Satan must get man to agree with evil ideas to be able to destroy you and others. Wrong choices give each person bad consequences.

The realm within the thousands of probabilities' given in our freewill choices in our life is what creates our physical <u>earthly destiny</u> and the Supernatural realm held within our Godly choices in our life creates our eternal <u>heavenly destiny</u>. Plus, Godly choices here on earth stops Satan from harming us and others.

Some people think they can call upon the dead to speak to them. The Lord says this is witchcraft and sorcery. However, you can say whatever you want to say to your loved ones, and they can hear you; so, tell them you love them. We human-beings created in God's image are Saints. We have different powers than angels. I have had experiences whereas a saintly image or a feeling of truth and a comforting message from a loved one who passed on did come to me and other family members. Remember, *<u>Matt 17:2</u>* . God showed us this power when Moses and Elijah appeared with Jesus before the disciples. However, do not think that the spirit of your loved one will ever move through another person to speak to you. The only one speaking to you from the spiritual realm from heaven is the Trinity within the Holy Spirit of truth. The Holy Spirit speaks to you and your loved ones about who you are in being a renewed creation in Christ's salvation, redemption, authority *(<u>Matt.6:10)</u>* "here on earth as it is in heaven". Your loved ones in the heavenlies are praying for you and worshipping the Trinity. Jesus and the Father *hears their petitions* and sends the Holy Spirit energy empowerment to the earth, a conduit to assist you in your every need and request when you choose to listen to the Spirit of Truth. We as saints have power also in the Holy Spirit. So, you may have a visitation from a loved one but it never comes to you from another person. That is Satan's trickery.

Satan and the demons only speak to your natures of the flesh. Satan uses people who agree with its lusts to manipulate them and others. *(<u>1ˢᵗ Peter 5:8)</u>* The Devil roams the earth seeking to destroy.

 GET THIS NOW! (*<u>Matt 6:9-13</u> The Lord's Prayer*):"On earth as it is in heaven." Our loved ones in heaven are living a supreme life full of being creative and joyful. They worship, praise, and prayerfully work as truly pure Saints in the heavenlies, perpetually growing in Christ likeness.

***With authority and boldness, we <u>speak your word Lord discerning</u> all that we do <u>each day.</u> <u>We are to learn how to separate our flesh nature from hindering who we really are through</u> <u>utilizing your power, LORD, within our spirit being. That is where our divine wisdom, true</u> <u>fellowship, anointed worship, pure righteousness, and real Holy Spirit empowerment comes</u> <u>from. So many Christians just want to stay complacent in living their Christian faith by</u> <u>a flesh understanding, instead of allowing Christ empowerment to flow in HIS perfection</u> <u>through us; ***as we are created to be "The Temple of the Holy Spirit..."</u> *John 16:13.* "When the Spirit of Truth comes, He will guide you in all truth."

***<u>*Ephesians 6:14,*</u> "We stand therefore having belted our loins with truth." This truth is evident in the gifts that you graciously give us Lord. We desire to have <u>fellowship with you,</u> JESUS that we may hear you and, become <u>anointed by the Holy Spirit to **"walk by the Spirit and live by the Word of God**</u> within each circumstance in our life". {In 1970, The Lord told this to me the 3ʳᵈ time I was spiritually taken to a heavenly place. Supernatural power, perpetual divine love, joy, peace and wisdom is gained when the flesh cannot influence us. Then we become truly empowered by being "holy whole" in our spirit being recreated in God's image.} Understand the depth of who you truly are in your spirit to override the natures of the flesh.

We must choose to recognize, utilize, and exercise YOUR WORD, Lord. We have truth with,

***__1st Cor.12:4-12__ "revelation, prophesy, wisdom, discernment, casting out evil, prayer language, interpretation of prayer language, healing and effecting of miracles."** These are the gifts that you, Lord, give us. So, as we can become proficient in them by different degrees at different times for ourselves, family, friends, loved ones and ministry tools to guide our life to successfully stay on the path that you have anointed for us to walk. This is so different from where the natures of the flesh want to take us. We praise you Lord for these amazing tools and spiritual insights that help guide us daily here on earth. {We are responsible and need to teach our children these powers in Christ. So, as they can cast out the evil in any gunman in their schools; because Satan must flee when we in Christ command him to flee by the name of Jesus!} **__Proverbs 18:10__ "The name of the Lord is a strong fortress; the godly run to him and are safe!" __Mark 16:17,18__ "In My name, (Jesus said) you will cast out demons and they will flee." We hold the power!**

I have had several personal experiences in my life whereas evil men were stopped by a Godly force before they could harm me. So, I know how powerful the action of casting evil off a person is truly effective. I had a blind date that went crazy in my home. He grabbed me by my throat, choking me, dragging me to my bed. He kept screaming, "I am raping you. I get what I want when I want it!" While he was choking me his knee went into my chest and his other hand-held my two wrists down on the bed.

I felt like my life was leaving me as I could not breathe!! On the brink of blacking out the Lord spoke to me, "Cross your legs now, now!" (I was very limber and very thin and when exercising I could wrap my leg around my neck), so by a miracle I gained strength to lift my leg not blocked by his body on top of me. As my foot with a black 5" stiletto heel came up almost to my head. He took his hand off of my throat and grabbed my shoe taking it off, then he ripped my other shoe off. I started grasping for air feeling death leave me and gaining my strength once again: as he loosens his belt and started to go to his zipper still screaming: A red gleam of lustful fire appeared in his eyes, as he repeated, "I am raping you." As he fumbled with his zipper, I ripped my hands away from his death grip: my wrist's had blood dripping from the cuts his nails made on them. One big breath I took as I screamed pointing my finger at him, "I command by the name of Jesus, you foul spirit get off, get off him NOW. I am the temple of the Holy Spirit, and I will not be defiled! 75,000 angels fill this room now!!!" A supernatural force picked him up and threw him across the room as he did a whiplash motion with his neck; stunned for a few seconds then he ran into my dressing room that led to a bathroom. I escaped harm and got him out of my house by a miracle from God. There is much more to this 1983 incident and what happened to him later that is told in my book about my life experiences.

We worship you, Immanuel and thank you for Life everlasting as given through the covenant you first made with Abraham. _Genesis 17._ **Which created the path in this divine covenant for our Redeemer's birth giving us, mankind back pureness through "Christ, The Savior," Our Redemption from the bad consequence of Adam's disobedience!**

*** We now, in the Trinity excel within a supernatural divine wisdom, true fellowship, anointed worship, pure righteousness, and a real empowerment in the Holy Spirit energy.

Help keep us attuned to you, Lord. As you have said, **we have authority** _Matt: 16:19; I will give you the keys to heaven … whatever you loose from Heaven will be loosen on earth_ _Matt 6:10_ **in the name of Jesus to bring heaven to earth.** _Matt. 28:18-20 , John 20: 19-24_ **"As the Father has sent me, even so I am sending you. Receive the HOLY SPIRIT"** As he comes from heaven to earth.

As in ***_Phil 4: 8_ … **"whatsoever things are of a good report (the A + for what we need to happen in our life); list all needs_____ 'Lord, if there be any virtue, and any praise,'" may the thoughts of our mind, passions of our heart and words within our actions only dwell on these anointed ideas. The Holy Spirit speaks to us. It is important to seek fellowship with other believers to have agreement in our prayers.** _Duet 32:30_ **"two believers agreeing in prayer will put 10,000 angels to flight." Also. in** _Matt 18:19-20_ "for where two or more are gathered in my name, I thy, Lord God, I am with you." The Trinity is with us in prayer.

The Lord, in "The Trinity" has guided me through many difficulties by answering my prayers! I have received many miracle healings in my life through prayers. One example is in 1985 when I was pregnant with Chrystall. In September, I had four impacted wisdom teeth, my face was swollen, and I was in a lot of pain. The dentist told me he could not do anything because I was six months pregnant. If he disturbed my wisdom teeth the infection might go through to the baby, and he could not give me any pain pills either. I went home praying "Lord, help me through this!" I called my friend, Sally Lanivich, she was a lay reader at Aiko Horman's ministries, I asked her to come over to my home with a few prayer warriors after their meeting. They came, they held my hands, and we agreed in prayer, "Christ Healing power will take the infection and the pain away amen!" Many scriptures were said, and we rejoiced in Christ healing powers. In the morning my swelling was gone, and I was in no pain at all. I rejoiced praising Jesus for my healing. I never had pain with my wisdom teeth again; even when months later I went to the dentist via my mother In-law's advice, (months after Chrystall was born) to get those wisdom teeth removed. Yes, all four at once and it didn't even hurt afterwards. Praise the Lord.

***Daily we ask forgiveness of our sins. We desire to walk in virtue, power, and authority with _Eph. 6:14,_ **the Breastplate of righteousness.** _Isaiah 61:10_ **God has arrayed me in HIS robe of righteousness;** _Lam. 3:22-23_ **because** of the Lord 's great Love we are not consumed; _Rev21:11_ **The Glory of God is the most precious brilliance. We are clothed in the garment of God's Glory** and that is fresh and new each day. Thank you, Jesus, for your grace, mercy, and forgiveness.

We desire to be obedient to you, Lord Jesus and hear your truth. We choose to cast out daily the evil within and around us. ***We take authority over the natures of the flesh that come within us to manipulate us taking us down a false path away from your divine will for our life. **We are**

all born this way, it is called, SIN and it is up to us to command these harmful natures in the flesh to flee from us, including our family, friends, loved ones, their loved ones and <u>all whom cross our paths friend or foe.</u> We command these natures to flee from us all *****_Gal.5:19-21,26_ "**
ego, envy, greed, pride; worry, fear, guilt; gossip, contrariness, orneriness, stubbornness; skepticism, criticism, negativity; procrastination, irresponsibility, impatience, distraction; vengeance, jealousy, covet-ness, stealing, hatred, anger, murder; drunkenness, carousing, adultery; idolatry, sorcery, philosophies of the world; judgmental attitudes, condemnation, self- centeredness, self- righteousness, self-destruction, generational curses; illness, injury illness, biochemical illness, all disease, all sexual perversion's especially, for the masochists, and sadomasochist."

We are all born this way; and it is _definitely called "Sin_," so by you, Jesus, raised from the dead, we are free. So, all harmful flesh natures must flee from all of us, _even unto our enemies_. Satan must get a human to agree with wicked ideas before Satan can do any evil. ***_Isaiah 54:17: "F_or no weapon formed against us will ever prosper." _Matt. 7:2._ **We all sin, do not judge another; for as you judge you will be judged. Yet, the truth must be revealed!**

Each one of us has many issues, which we must deal with daily. When understanding the natures of the flesh we can easily say with a tone of self-righteousness, "oh I don't do that!" Oh, Lord, Gee, I guess it is so easy for us to think we are so perfect. When in our reality, it is easy to see where we are good and not so easy to see our faults; when it is our weaknesses in the thorn in the flesh, that we must battle with daily. We all justify the things in the flesh. God, you know how our thorn in our side is the natures of flesh which are also, those things that are the hardest for us to control. God, you forgive us, but we can never say it is not sin just because we want to live in it. We understand Lord the freedom in forgiveness through Salvation and do not judge another's walk within you, Christ, The Savior. Matt. 7:3 "why do you look at the speck in another's eye when you have a plank in your own!" Fault finding is always destructive. God wants us to pray for each other not condemn each other.

WE ARE PURPOSED BY OUR REDEMPTION TO RECOGNISE THE NATURES OF THE FLESH MOVING THOUGH US AND CAST THEM OUT IMMEDIATELY.

Gossip is equal and the same as murder, most of us live in-between. WHY? Any sin separates us from your fellowship Lord! _Roman's 7:19, 20_ "For I do not do the good I want, but the evil I do not want is what **I** keep on doing. Now, if I do that which I should not. It is no more I that do it, but the sin which dwells within me." The flesh has power, which is why <u>we must daily build up who we are in Spirit,</u> not forgetting about our power in salvation. Satan pushes us into condemnation, I have been there done that! God, you set us free through Christ Jesus and the anointing of the Holy Spirit!

VICTORY OVER EVIL THROUGH THE SCRIPTURES:

Thee, Lord, God Almighty, your only plan for our redemption from Adam's disobedience is Christ salvation. *Matt. 16:23 when evil attacks,* just say what Christ said when Peter was moving in the flesh, instead of the spirit of truth, "Get behind me, Satan! You are a stumbling block to me, you do not have in mind the concerns of God, but merely human concerns. (Peter)" Satan fuels our flesh concerns, which are against God's concerns.

As we stand firm with ******Ephesians 6:15* "our feet shod in the preparation of the gospels of peace." Allow the Holy Spirit to guide you whenever you speak, and you will find favor.** We choose to embrace these fruits from heaven <u>and do not distinguish them by the ways of the world.</u> *****Gal.5:22-25** Jesus empowers us in each moment with His **divine supernatural omnibenevolent, "love, joy, peace, patience, gentleness, kindness, faithfulness, goodness and spiritual self-control."** May these spiritual fruits flow freely through us within all circumstances of the day, we receive this and are empowered by you, Jesus. **We do not condemn others. God loves us all and we are to love all. Praise the Lord. "The greatest of these is God's love."** 1st *Cor. 13:4--8, 13 Forgiveness is so important to grow in a Holy Spirit anointing. John 20:21-23*

****Ephesians 6:16, "Above all taking the shield of faith where with we will be able to extinguish all of the fiery darts of the wicked." Take notice, Satan and the third of the host of <u>Demon angels;</u> you can no longer empower this evil unto man. God Almighty gave us tremendous power to stop wickedness if we choose to use HIS power to do so. There is much more to the story of *Job 1:8 -10 Job was a man who had abundant blessings from God Almighty. He had a reverence toward God and he is very protected by a great hedge that stopped Satan from harming him.* **When Satan approached God about how everyone sins. God responded, "Hast thou considered my servant Job, that there is none like him in the earth, a perfect and an upright man, one who has a reverent honor towards God and avoids evil."**

Satan replied, " ..Thou has put a hedge around him and all that he has. And, then blessed all in his life increasing his substance greatly. If I take all that away Job will curse you God." Job lost everything yet still honored the Lord through his losses. This is a good lesson.

I stop the story here because when I asked God, "why did you take the hedge away from Job? Lord, you knew that the probability of Satan asking for that removal of the hedge was an option in your laws in the universe and that consequences come from our choices in life! Tell me more about this hedge Lord tell me more! Why did you first place the hedge around Job; when you knew you would be taking it away?"

***The Lord answered me, "yes, my precious child there is much more, I placed that hedge around Job knowing that the day Satan asked me to remove it from Job WAS THE DAY that

gave you my children the total right to place a HOLY HEDGE AROUND ANYONE WHO YOU WANT TO STOP SATAN FROM FUELING THEIR NATURE'S IN THE FLESH WITH EVIL IDEAS. *** 'Yes, everyone from loved ones to evil ones trying to hurt you; place my Holy Hedge around them and this stops Satan from enslaving them to do evil works. We must cast Satan out every time evil tries to manipulate us with the natures of the flesh. Yes, each person will still have freewill, but they are not a slave to Satan's ideas.' Also, know that this hedge shows us, as Christ Saints, that when we place that Holy Hedge, we, and our loved ones will have abundant blessings to enhance our lives just as Job's life was enhanced by having a Godly hedge around him."

Romans 6:14- 17 "Sin is still your enemy and tempts you, in the easiest ways but you are no longer enslaved to sin." *** Since Christ coming and ascending, we as God's children have a supernatural power to conquer the natures of the flesh in everyone around us. Place God's hedge around ourselves and loved ones to stop Satan from fueling our wickedness's and speak ***_phil. 4:8 the good report of what we want them to become. Stop condemning them to be enslaved to their weakness in the thorn in their side. Every time we speak in a negative way about anything in life, we give Satan power by agreeing with Satan about their weakness, so as our words will keep them enslaved. We must learn how to speak about our friends and family, the way Christ speaks about us to the Father through the HOLY SPIRIT ' we are Righteous and clean from our sins' Example:_ a person has won the battle over drug addition, stealing, greed, murder, illness, dementia, cancer, covid, vaccines, hatred, anger, vengeances, gossip, sexual perversions, and idolatry. ***_Proverbs 18:21_ "The tongue can make life or death." Whatever we speak, we reap that harvest in our life for ourselves and our loved ones. Christ gives His children a supernatural power to conquer the evil natures of the flesh in all circumstances in life. I say that from numerous experiences in my life whereas the power of God changed a bad consequence to a good or great consequence. In 1993, a man who (AT THE TIME I DID NOT KNOW) was Russian Mafia tried to harm me. He put a knife to my chin telling me, "I am going to chop you up piece by piece and then cut off your head. But first I am putting you in the party room downstairs and you will "service" everyone I send down there. You see I have a new bodyguard right! Well, no one will find the other bodyguard, and no one will find you either. Not the police, the FBI, or the CIA, no one"

God gave me a supernatural wisdom, emotional strength, clever wit, and _no fear,_ as he was saying these despicable words to me!!! I could not escape, all the doors and gates had security locks, and he had to push a certain button to allow anyone to leave the property. Oh, I started praying inside my mind, 'Lord, get me out of here'. God told me to go upstairs to finish arranging the accessories in the home. By the anointing of the Holy Spirit in me which was more powerful than Satan in him I walked out of there unharmed. This whole story is truly compelling on how I escaped and what happened to him later. All events will be told in detail in my autobiography.

God's word is omnipotent, omniscient, omnipresent, and proven for us by the centurion soldier, who came seeking Christ to heal his servant who was ill at home. _Matt. 8:5-13_ the soldier said, "Lord, just say the word for that is good enough to heal my servant. Lord, you do not have to go there to my home. I am a man of authority who tells his servant, 'Do this and he does it' a man of authority is obeyed. You, Lord, and your words are the authority to heal my servant. {Speak the word for it is Omnipotent, Omnipresent and Omniscient}

Jesus responded, "Truly I tell you; I have not found anyone in Israel with such great faith. _Matt 8:13_ "Go! Let it be done just as you believe it would." The servant was healed.

John 14:12-28 Christ sent the Holy Spirit to empower us. We have Christ authority in us and are very powerful if we use His words. So, stop giving Satan power, especially in exercising. Yoga is a ritual of Satan to worship the flesh. (_The. Hindu, Buddha yoga is 1st mentioned in ancient religious text of "Rig Vedas" and derives from ancient Indian spiritual practices and an explicitly religious element. Mantras are repetitive sounds used to penetrate the depths of the unconscious mind and adjust the vibration of all aspects of your being. Remember, Mantras can be chanted or just listened to._) You open yourself up to the evil spirits of the universe going into the core of your subconscious. Making it harder for you to recognize the generational curses in the natures of the flesh. The poses are postures of animals & plants to worship the earth and Satan. God Almighty has instructed us in:

Col. 2:8 to flee from these things which create idol worship. There are other exercises which are more effective.

Karma is birthed into existence via Satan wanting us to be punished for our disobedience just as he is punished for his disobedience. Satan wants us to activate punishment upon mankind by us saying, "they'll get their karma for doing that!" We are cursing our loved ones by saying that. We are cursing our life when we believe in Karma. Because, as we condemn others to get a bad consequence for their wrong doings then we in turn allow Satan to give us a bad consequence for all our wrong choices. Karma is not used to give a blessing.

God wants us to rebuke evil not activate evil. _1st Peter3:9,_" Not returning evil for evil or insult for insult but giving a blessing instead; for you were called for the very purpose to pray for one another that you might inherit that blessing of Christ pure love." Oh, the joy of overcoming the natures of the flesh. We are in every circumstance purposed to rebuke and cast out Satan's evil ideas. Satan needs a human to do evil.

ONCE YOU RECEIVE CHRIST SALVATION, YOU ARE A RENEWED CREATURE IN CHRIST'S REDEMPTION FULL OF DIVINE SUPERNATURAL POWERS

We are truly created once and have an eternity in either heaven or hell. It is our freewill choice. If we deny Christ and the Holy Spirit, we have inadvertently chosen hell. If we do not want to seek salvation, then we have allowed Satan to blind us. Christ is the only one who broke the curse of Adam's wrong choice that gave mankind a very bad consequence. Christ is making a new creation in us with his new covenant whereas we gain the blessings. In His salvation even though we have made some wrong choices and have sinned God still wants to bless us showing us how not to keep making wrong choices. We are the only creation made in God's image. We have a freewill choice for salvation and redemption.

We, being believers in Christ have power in the Holy Spirit anointing to stop Satan from enslaving people. The following we are to say daily to stop Satan's fueling of these people's wicked natures of the flesh from enslaving people with Satan's evil ideas.

***We command the harmful natures of the flesh, Satan and all Demons to flee off of "ALL" Democrats, Republicans, RINOs, Liberals, Communist, Independents, Marxist, Socialists, Protesters, Terrorists, Vandalistic Rioters, Suicidal & Mentally ill people; Drug makers, dealers, addicts, Gang members, Murderers, Thieves; Pimps, Pornographers, Prostitutes, Strippers, Pedophiles', Sexual traffickers, Rapists, all whom practice sexual perversions,' and all Idolaters, Atheists, Agnostics, Hindus, Buddhist, Islamist, Satanists are set free. In addition, **all Christians and Jews are free from these evils. By the blood of JESUS,** I say you, Satan, Demons, and the evil harmful natures of the flesh; you can no longer empower these people to do these evil works.

If every Christian would rebuke Satan and the natures of the flesh each time wicked ideas would come into our head or by seeing evil actions of another person: If these were rebuked with saying, **"by the name of Jesus you foul spirits are command to flee"** _Matt 16:23_ **"Get behind me Satan."** We would truly experience a new world around us.

James 1:13-14 "Let no man say when he is tempted, 'I am tempted by God'; for God cannot be tempted by evil, and he, himself does not tempt anyone. Each one is tempted when he is carried away by his own lust." I pray they will no longer lust after or gain satisfaction from these evil ideas. I pray a "Saul to Damascus" experience for these non-believers to gain a changed life!

Jesus, your Salvation sets man apart from this evil. Jesus, you empower and redeem us giving us wisdom via the Holy Spirit. Lord let your gifts given to each man manifest to all

good things for each person to realize who we truly are created to be unique and special. ***_John 3:17_ "God did not send Jesus into the world to condemn it but that all might be saved."** We are empowered to overcome the natures of the flesh; to be anointed by you, Jesus via the Holy Spirit, Pure in God's eyes. <u>We Receive and We Believe we are redeemed Saints in Christ.</u>

Bless our nation with goodness. **We pray passionately for the entertainment industry and news media on all levels; to know you, JESUS, and turn from their wicked ways of advocating all evil works within this nation. Mankind's harmful flesh natures are fed and fueled by immorality especially, feeding the flesh to desire evil over good. (Fuel: is a source of stimulation; "something that stimulates or maintains something else <u>especially emotions</u>")**

Lord, bless the entertainment industry with righteousness, to model good values and morals to encourage the viewers to empower their life with goodness, decency, integrity, and joy. Feeding and strengthening the spirit man to power. To recognize goodness for goodness and evil for evil and not be desensitized to truth. The producing of Soap Operas created more divorces in America than any time before. Violence in video games created more violence in some of our kids. The wicked word's in music gives children despair. We God's saints must teach our children the truth. _1st Cor. 3:16_ , "Do you not know that you are God's temple and that God's spirit dwells in you." The Trinity empowers God's children.

Bless us Lord with,***_Ephesians 6:17,_ **"the Helmet of Salvation"** Salvation is as stated in _John 3:16,_ **"God so loved the world that he gave his only begotten son, _(so that His first creation born in His image, 'MAN' could gain back eternal life in His blessed kingdom)._** When we believe in Jesus as Lord and ask forgiveness of our sins and know that only you, LORD JESUS, rose from the dead as our savior; we are saved. _John 3:17_ God did not send Jesus into the world to condemn the world, but in order that the world might be saved through him." You promised us Lord in _Acts 16:31;_ you and your household will be saved. (NOTE)

It is important to understand that when Lucifer rebelled in heaven, God knew that was one of several choices for Lucifer, and the consequence was Lucifer was being thrown out of heaven to earth, taking 1/3 of the angels out of heaven. These angels are demons now. Transformed by the laws of consequences. If you make wrong choices, you get bad consequences.

<u>God knew if his original creation of man being created in God's image was ever to fail also, that he would have a backup plan for mankind's redemption. Christ salvation circumvents the bad consequences from Adam's wrong disobedient choice.</u> God Almighty told us so when Abraham was sacrificing Isaac, _Genesis 22:2-13,_ "The Lord will provide" (the sacrifice.)

Consider these facts, God created all the animals both male and female. _Genesis 2:7_ Then when he created man in his image; _**he blew the Holy Spirit into Adam giving exceptional life.**_ One unique creation is woman, _Genesis 2:21-22_ as God took a part of man to create woman. I asked God, "Why did you do that? You could have created woman the same as you created man! You created all the other animals, male and female the same way, the same time!" **While in deep prayer, God revealed to me** (*Eph 6:19*) **"a mystery revelation."** He took a part of man to create woman and justifiably so; as He had to **take a part of himself to create Jesus {THE WORD OF CREATION} and God Almighty also, took another part of himself {that gave the energy empowerment} creating the Holy Spirit.** So God had the prior knowledge of the possibility that Adam might fail thus giving Satan the right to give mankind the natures of the flesh along with death in Hell; thus, taking God's most precious creation "mankind", allowing them to be tortured! God planned a redeemer so mankind could be saved. (*Genesis 3:15*) **"The seed of the women will bruise His heel while crushing Satan's head"** By the way, man has more power than Satan ever will have however, Satan can control man through the natures of the flesh, destroying man in God's image by man choosing to give up God's powers.

God loves mankind so much that he knew if Adam failed him; then He could take that part of himself **which created Jesus Christ in the beginning; {THE WORD OF CREATION}** just as after God blew the Holy Spirit upon Adam then he took a part of man to make woman to utilize these two unique creations to give mankind back redemption. This allows man to be in fellowship with God again and go to a Heavenly eternity with him. Jesus is born of the flesh to be "The Savior" bringing the Holy Spirit empowerment energy to mankind to conquer the evil in man.

John 1:1-3 **" In the beginning was the word, and the word was with God, and the word was God. He 'Christ' was in the beginning with God and all things were made through him."** The word of creation. (We are recreated in Christ to be renewed in God's image)

2nd Cor 5:19 **"to wit, that God was in Christ, reconciling the world unto himself, not imputing their trespasses unto them; and hath committed unto us the word of reconciliation."** God did send himself as the deliverer. **That is why it is not about religion; it is about God's plan for man's redemption; Christ is THE Savior. The only redeemer of mankind. Idolatry will fill your flesh with satisfactions in religious rituals of the flesh that only hinder your true power in living in Christ a supernatural divine spiritual life.**

Lord, this salvation is not just for the rights of a blessed eternity but for salvation over all that we do this day in our work and in our play. We pray for salvation **blessings over the air that we breathe, water and fluids we drink, all foods we eat, all paper and plastic products we use daily plus, all electronics, the machines that we use and the energy that gives the power.** Protect us Jesus from the things of the world that can harm us. LORD, you said, ******Mark 16:17-18 "that we could pick up any poisonous thing and that it would not harm us." The harmful things in this world are sometimes the synthetic chemicals in our air, foods, liquids, medicines, lotions, cleaning supplies, paper goods plus, all machines, cell phones and computer electronics etc. Therefore, we take authority and pray a protection for us even though we must use these things; your blood, Jesus, divinely protects us, internally and externally. Lord, your energies are more powerful than evil. *eph.6:10-19* **"Holy armor."** *1st Thes 5:16* Pray over everything never ceasing. When we ask for your guidance in all that we do. ***Lord, send Holy Angels to purify everything***

around and inside our loved ones and ourselves..

<u>Jesus, give us restoration over our health and wellbeing. Say whom you wish to pray for: _____</u>We know we sin, error, and make mistakes when falling short in our life choices. We thank you, Jesus, for guiding us through those errors in life. We receive your forgiveness for our sins. As You Lord guide us to a much better life. ***<u>Hosea 4:6 "My people will perish for lack of knowledge."</u> <u>We are to educate ourselves about the things around us. Vet the people we meet.</u> ***<u>Kindly pray for all who are dysfunctional, and enslaved to wickedness.</u>***

A few times in my life; I have not listened when God was warning me to not to do something and I got a bad consequence from being disobedient. Back in 1981, I sometimes did not know the true voice of the Lord. This time I thought it was Satan telling me to flee from this man, who had received Jesus Christ into his life and was going with me to 4 church services each Sunday: Hal Lindsey 6am, Bel Air Presbyterian 11am, The Vineyard 4pm and Church on the Way 6pm, and 3 bible studies a week …I got engaged to him and we went to the marriage counselling classes at The Vineyard. This story is long and very intricate to the many incidents that happened which led up to me getting a restraining order against him. The Marshall and the private eye could not find him to serve the papers…Genevieve Segura, my dearest friend, since high schools days came to stay with me for a few days on her way to China.

She looks a lot like Jaclyn Smith of "Charlie's Angels." So, I asked her to be with my angels guiding me to serve Isaac the restraining order papers. I had only one day left to serve him the papers or I would have to pay $1,500 for new papers to file with the court.

Gen hesitated at first for a few reasons, number one she was traveling and didn't want to get involved but came on board when I told her, "God is going to divinely guide me to where he is today!"

We both were laughing as she said, "Ok Linda if you can find him, I will serve the papers."

I prayed for The Lord to forgive me when 3 x 3 times, I did not listen when God warned me "Flee from this man" I thought, 'Lord I really believed he loves you and received salvation and that it was Satan trying to hurt him if I left him. So, I Pray you give me favor this day Lord and guide me to him so Gen can serve these papers. I am an innocent victim, Lord; I am an innocent victim with a pure heart! Help Me Jesus! Please guide me to him.'

Genny and I set out on our adventure to pick up the papers at the attorney's office Mid-Wilshire district in LA. After leaving the attorney we had driven about 20 minutes when Genny desperately apologizing asked to go back to the shop where we got flowers as a prop to fool Isaac when she served him. She left her sunglasses there and needed them for her trip,

The shop was closed but through frantic knocking and eyeglass motions, as the clerk was saying, "no, we are closed": finally, he came to the door and gave her the sunglasses.

I kept saying, "Praise the Lord we are in God's perfect timing, all is well!" driving for about two hours after leaving the house, we combed the streets of LA making every turn believing God was guiding me. We came to the corner of 3rd St and Robertson Blvd. I said, "Genny duck down now," she crouched her tall slender body down into the small front seat of my 450 SL Mercedes. I made a right turn and then two more right turns going down a parking lot alleyway behind some stores, slowly driving scanning the area intensely believing with all my heart that he was there somewhere!! But to my dismay I said. "ahhhh, Genny, get up! I really felt like the Lord was telling me, he is here. Yet he is nowhere to be found." She sat up. I looked both ways as I was going to make a left turn back unto 3rd St. securing my turn I looked right again and noticed a panel truck pulling away from the gas pump at the corner gas station and to my surprise I screamed, "Genny I can't believe it .. Ahhhh! There he is pumping gas at that gas pump over there!!!!" She got out of the car and walked up to Isaac and served the papers. He turned white as a ghost, and I felt the hand of God upon me telling me to fear not any longer… There are compelling facts to this relationship of how this con man used me, took $35,000.00 from me, and disparaged my name to make himself look good to those he was probably using also! The documented facts are in my autobiography. When we call upon the Lord, he will guide us through our despair in life bringing us favor.

Lord God Almighty, you tell us in ***Psalms 32:8 "I will instruct, teach and guide you." We desire your divine protection and guidance this day. We pray for sweet traveling mercies for us, plus all mentioned in this prayer, including our family, friends, and loved ones. ***Teach us Lord to hear your voice and recognize our obedience within your guidance. Show us how to flee the harmful natures of the flesh. **Holy, warring, and ministering Angels, by the anointing of Jesus through the Holy Spirit, go forth now and assist in the needs on all levels everyone mentioned in this prayer. Amen, we have faith.** When we pray for others and ourselves, Lord, give that mustard seed of faith that you gifted each human being with upon their creation, the power to hear your truth, so as we grow in faith. _Matt 17:20-21_ "Faith the size of a mustard seed." Nothing is impossible when the smallest mustard seed grows fast into a tall 30' tree. A little faith applied is fast to grow giving a Holy Spirit power to the fullest degree of necessity for our needs.

One Nation Under God

***Lord, especially, bless our Nation, as we are a Judeo-Christian Nation, show our President, Congress, Executive, Legislative, and Judicial branches of government and all who serve in our nation; that we must adhere to the religious moral valves of our Judeo-Christian Bible to survive and to continue to be a blessed nation. If the leaders of our nation cannot do this, then replace them with someone who will do your will GOD. As our founding forefathers of our Constitution stated insistently, that this document would fail if we deviated from these values.

Ideas as the same used in how a Social Security number works in our State/Federal government can be utilized in a way to have a State/Federal Voter ID.

The Lord gives us, the patriots, the means to stop all fraudulent voters that defile our votes as citizens. Any person who has an agenda to destroy our Constitution or our Bill of Rights should never ever even be placed on any government position ballot in America. We can ask why? Because they would never uphold or abide by our Constitution or our Bill of Rights which is important criteria for anyone to hold any government position in America. We the patriots must stand up and care about our nation. Call congress 202 224 3121 give your zip code to be directed to your representatives and senators. Leave a message to let them know that we as citizens do not want our votes to be defiled in our state and federal elections! We demand voter re-registration of all citizens with proof of citizenship, birth certificate, legal address, photo ID, fingerprints, and a chip with all this information placed into a new State/Federal voter ID card. Each ballot would come with a fingerprint kit for each voter to be verified, then all elections will be accurate. This is not prejudicial because if a person cannot figure out how to register then how in the world would they ever be capable of voting. We the people must stop the issues of dead people, felons, illegal immigrants, stop cross county and state line triple voting practices, Plus, stop fake mail in ballots not vetted like the absentee ballots must be to mail in the votes. ***This is the most economical, effective and efficient way to stop voter fraud in America.*** The people who object to this voter ID are the people who most likely would commit voter fraud. One more thing: when you call congress tell them that there must be stronger laws to prosecute voter fraud with high fines, jail time and losing their right to vote in the future for anyone caught committing voter fraud. **Why would any citizen want to object to these secure criteria!**

Our founding forefathers created A Bible Society to place a bible in every school so as our nation's children would grow up learning the scriptures; to empower their life, to be better leaders for America's future. They said, "It should be Christians' in our government positions to ensure America's enduring blessed future." Lord, bring our NATION BACK to THESE VALUES. Jesus, we need the Bible put back into our public school system; with open prayer honored as our religious right in this great nation. Christ salvation is the only way to conquer evil.

The separation of Church and State was created to stop the government from taking away our Christian rights in public places. When our founders were creating our Bill of Rights and our Constitution back in England it was the practice that if a King was Catholic everyone had to be Catholic and if the King was Protestant, then everyone had to be Protestant. Our Founding Forefathers did not want government control over our religious practices. Our government officials in the 60's started bamboozling our citizens by taking prayer out of our public schools.

Our Nation was the first to establish the freedom of PRAYER. The Puritans in 1600 taught the bible in public schools. Our founding forefathers established "The Northwest Ordinance 1787" to further Bible education in our public schools to teach our religious rights for all people to understand about our <u>freedom rights to know about salvation.</u>

<u>Lord, stop the Muslims, Communist, Marxist, Atheists and Socialists from destroying America. Some choose Hell by a freewill choice. *** these people who have rejected salvation have no right to take Christ salvation knowledge away from others; so, as they can ALSO make a freewill choice based upon the value of being presented the truth about Christ redemption. Which empowers believers with the Holy Spirit anointing which conquers the evil natures of the flesh and breaks the curse of death in Hell. Salvation births into each person a new creation of power in the Trinity by being anointed by {The Word of Creation} CHRIST, and {the supernatural energy empowerment of} THE HOLY SPIRIT. We are Saints with authority in Christ righteousness in us.</u>

<u>In Christ 2nd coming, he gives us a new earth where no evil will be thwarting mankind. *2nd Peter 3:13 "according* to HIS promise we are looking for a new heaven and a new earth, in which righteousness dwells."</u> Pure righteousness can never be found in the flesh here on earth **unless it is pure only in Christ by the anointing of the Holy Spirit.** <u>Which gives believers, who are saints in Christ redemption, a spiritual advantage over evil here on earth when we apply his word. Those who live by religious rituals only truly satisfy their own natures of the flesh, which thwart the Holy Spirit manifesting within their life.</u> **<u>We are Mighty, Worthy, Worker, Warrior, Saints in Christ, and the Holy Spirit anointing in Christ here on earth and in heaven. We are mighty soldiers in Christ kingdom to do His work here on earth. We are responsible to stop evil here on earth. God gave us the powers to do so.</u>**

WE ARE WORTHY WORKER WARRIOR SAINTS IN CHRIST REDEMPTION

Bless our active, inactive, retired military and all our military leaders plus our allied military, close by and around the world. Bless them and give them supernatural wisdom in all that they do. The Holy Spirit empowerment will anoint them that they may escape evil by seeing clearly and supernaturally the acts of the enemy before any evil can attack them.

Lord, **help us all in this world especially, Christians, Jews, and Israelites to have a spiritual boldness in finding the terrorist in each of our nations and bringing those terrorists to justice. Bless Israel** *1st Peter 2:9* **and** help your nation's people with seeing clearly that you, Lord Jesus, are the LORD of Salvation for the whole world. **Genesis 12 & 17** Abram heard your voice LORD, and then you created the Hebrews to pave the path of "The Savior" for **(John3:17)** the salvation of the whole world. Save our Israel and bring the borders back to your kingdom plan. Bless us Jesus, YHWH, Elohim, El Shaddai, Adonai, Immanuel, Jehovah, Jehovah Rapha, with righteousness. ***You, Lord, personally speak to the spirit of every human. You, Lord, give us freewill &**

LIFE. When we choose your plan for redemption, we conquer evil.

I have many real-life experiences whereas I spoke the word of God and evil men were thrown across the room by warring angels, and those men could no longer try, and harm me. We need to make it a priority to teach our youth the true empowerment of Christ in us. In every school shooting if one person would have just said, "You foul evil spirit on this gunman, you are commanded to flee from them now; by the power of Christ word in me, evil must flee from you now. I am the temple of the Holy Spirit in Christ and Satan, and all cohorts must obey and flee now. 75,000 warring angels fill this room now" They would have been stopped from their hypnotism desire to kill innocent people. Christ stops evil.

We have, Lord, ***_Ephesians 6:17,_ **"The Sword of the Spirit, in our hands, which is the word of God"** : _Hebrews 4:12_ _"God's word is alive and active. Sharper than a two-edged sword, it divides soul and spirit; it judges the thoughts and attitudes of the heart"._

Isaiah 55:11 **"God's WORD will not return void unto him but shall accomplish all that it is purposed to achieve we will go out with joy and be led forth by peace."** You, Lord, will bless and protect us all the days of our life when we live through your salvation, we conquer evil.

Proverbs 3:5, 6 **"We lean not unto our own understanding but in all thy ways we acknowledge you Lord, that you make straight and direct our paths."** Even though we have some daily conflicts here on earth, there is a great blessing held within the conflict for those who love the Lord. ***_Romans 8:28_ **"**All things work together for good to them who love the Lord and are called according to HIS purpose." (God's purpose is) ***_1st Thessalonians 5:16-18,_

"that we pray over everything never ceasing." 'Lord be with me in this that I do'

We gain divine energy through _worship, fellowship, praise, and trust in Christ by asking for His help. We have Joy in all things. If you have fear, anger or hatred you give Satan power to make things worse. Satan tries to kill us but when you agree with Satan, evil leads you to hurt yourself. It is written in the laws of consequences. When we call upon Christ, we have victory._

We are in a spiritual war however, Jesus, you guide us through it; so, we must stay steadfast. Daily we pray for all MANKIND, all trades people in every profession: all workmen, teachers, scientist, inventors, military, police, fireman, paramedics, healthcare practitioners,' nutritionists', dentist, doctors, nurses, anesthesiologist, therapists, caregivers, agriculturist, manufacturers, corporations, sports, creative arts, artist, writers, directors, producers, actors, singers, government officials and all Christian ministers and all Christians. Lord, anoint all we do daily. _Psalms 32:8_ God instructs, teaches, and guides us in all our endeavors. All other religions are not in the Trinity. Most religions tell you that you must earn your right to go to heaven; through doing good works depriving yourself of things you sacrifice to make yourself righteous. These religions take portions of God's scriptures and distort the true meaning within the real power The Trinity blesses each person with upon receiving salvation. Christ tells us just come to me I will show you the light through your troubled times.

HEALTH AND SUCCESS

***Phil. 4:19* "Almighty God shall supply our every need according to HIS riches in Glory and those are vast and bountiful." We are very blessed spiritually, mentally, physically, emotionally, chemically, electrically, and financially. ***We call forth restoration of our health and wellbeing; that each cell of our bodies is conformed to the perfect-ness of God's purpose as by Christ our savior's salvation. ***Phil. 4:13* "We can do all things through Christ who strengthens us." We command our body to receive Christ supernatural healings.

***Ephesians 6:18,* "Praying always with all prayer and supplications in the Spirit, and watching thereunto with all perseverance and petitions for all saints" All people are Saints in Christ, *We are NOT ANGELS !* You demote our spiritual powers when you say a person is an angel. Angels never get the option for redemption from their disobediences. Satan loves it when his initial lie, "you will be like gods," is perpetuated by the mankind calling each other angels!!! Oh, Satan tells you it is just a saying of endearment. (Remember Satan is just an angel, who wanted to be like God, and "It" thought "It "would be; if "It" could overthrow God in the kingdom of heaven) If you as mankind believe you have no more power than angels then you will never be capable of exercising your true power of being created in God Almighty's image. We are Holy Saints in Christ redemption! Do you know who you are, try to Own Christ in you! We have more power than angels do. If a person has a given name of "Angel", they are not actually an angel. However, the name means "messenger of God." Demons lost the angel status. *All given birth names, and all words carry tremendous power in God's kingdom. Be very wise in what you say. Remember words created the heavens and earth. Also, words can create death of the mind, spirit, soul, and body.*

Josh 1: 8 "we shall mediate on the word of The Lord, our God Day and Night that we may be careful to do all that is accordingly written within it; for then we shall make our path prosperous and have good success." We pray primarily for **spiritual success** to have a timely word in a timely fashion for all who cross our path. For when we are blessed abundantly spiritually, we are blessed in all areas of life including business success and friendships everlasting.

***As in the *prayer of Jabez, 1ˢᵗ chronicles 4:10 "oh, Lord God of Israel, bless me, and all of my loved ones: increase* our territories, let your hand be with us and keep us from harm, so that we will be free from pain," Lord, anoint all business, career, and work we partake in bringing us financial rewards.** Give us favor among people to be chosen for the project at hand, for our path is enhanced. May all whom have met us remember us for future work in all areas of our talents. We are givers of the land and successful in all the gifts that you, Lord have set before us. Name your need here____ God supplies all our needs. *Phil 4:19*

Take care of your health and try not to put too many synthetic chemicals in your body. Read labels and Google words to know what the side effects can be. Write the side effects down. Get the app "YUKA". Stop buying products that have bad synthetic chemicals in them. Such as **all artificial sweeteners,** Aspartame, high fructose corn syrup, sodium nitrates, sodium nitrites, sodium benzoate, potassium benzoate, MSG, Canola oil, aka Rapeseed Oil, Palm oil, Calcium Carbonate, Dipotassium Phosphate, artificial food coloring red, yellow, blue dyes, butylated Hydroxyanisole BHA, GMO. Watch out for a synthetic process of organic foods and herbs that some of the vitamin industries are using such as Hypromelous fake gelatin, Medium chain triglycerides oil, microcrystalline cellulose, Magnesium stearate, calcium palitrate, these can cause nausea, and diarrhea plus other side effects that hurt our bodies. (Some processes and ingredients are manmade chemicals with no beneficial use, and they cause serious issues with our brains, heart, kidneys and liver.) Stop your ego wanting these products just because the item tastes good. Teach your tastebuds to enjoy new foods that are healthy; Learn what is harmful.

Vet all pharmaceutical drugs and really take heed to the side effects. Check out what is in the crèmes, lotions, skin products, hair products, deodorants, cleaning supplies plus laundry products which have bad synthetic chemicals that cause cancer and other diseases plus auto immune illness.

Hosea 4:6 My people will perish for lack of knowledge. {God gives us warnings through prophesy; so, as we can change the things that could be bad for us in our lifetime}

***We lift-up praise and worship to you, Lord Jesus and thank you daily for your grace and glory, which guides our life. **We pray for family, friends, loved ones, and ourselves.** As we all walk with great divine generational blessings. {we, are created in your image LORD God Almighty}. So we have a supernatural Godly courage, confidence; charisma, radiance, attraction, appeal; communication, conversation, comprehension skills, perception of all that is around us; (**seeing the good embracing it and recognizing the bad immediately , so as to cast it out, away from us and our loved ones daily)**; Anoint us with great short and long term memory and blessings in all that we do each day. You, Lord, enhance and bless us, and the lives around us. *Isaiah 41:13 "For I, the Lord thy God will hold thy right hand, saying into thee, fear not, I will help thee. Amen."*

Ephesians 6:19, **"for me, that utterance may be given unto me, that I may be bold to make known the mystery of the gospel."** All praise and glory to You, Lord Jesus, as we receive and believe, Jesus, you are The Lord who gives us back LIFE in an everlasting divine eternity in a supernatural love, comfort, joy, peace, and wisdom. As we are the temple of the Holy Spirit = Saint's in Christ here on earth and in heaven. *Matt.6:9-13* Again, I say we are not angels, but Satan was an angel that turned into a demon. **Satan can only have power if we give in to evil ideas or do not stop someone who has given in. Satan works at dummying down the mind of mankind. Taking away all knowledge of Christ in society , stops our freewill choice and enslaves mankind to perversions, lust, idolatry, greed, self-destructions, acts of murder, stealing and vandalism.**

All powerful LOVE of God Almighty is the omnibenevolent character of The Trinity.

Proverbs 3:5,6 Lean not unto your own understanding but in all thy ways acknowledge God and He will direct your path to success and prosperity. We have the power to give up Satan's wicked ideas that only bring us a temporal thrill or a short-term flesh satisfaction. Satan wants to dissect a human being into a scientific robot taking all Godly ideas out of earth.

God's ways are perpetually ever growing deeper in our lives evermore; when we choose to fellowship daily with Almighty God, Christ our Savor, and the Holy Spirit of truth: psalms 32:8 God instructs, teaches, and guides us daily.

By LindaJane Chapman via a Holy Spirit anointing

<u>Chapter 2</u>   "Why is it Important to Receive Christ Salvation Redemption?"

***The following are the true scriptures to help us, as Christ Saints, here on earth to share with others why it is so very important for their personal eternity to understand salvation redemption.

Satan is the one who condemns man to eternity in the sufferings of Hell. It is each man's free will choice. However, it is eternity whichever each man chooses. **<u>I champion each person to use scriptures daily when they pray and do not just give a moment of silence. Silence is void of all power.</u>** That is Satan's goal to make us powerless to his manipulations. Remember Satan lies in a very believable way. Satan fuels the natures of the flesh to desire satisfaction.

Speak God's word via Jesus "The Lord" as this conquers evil. All life and Glory to The Lord Jesus Christ, who gave us back redemption from the fall of Adam. <u>*John 8:58 Jesus*</u> said, "very truly I tell you, before Abraham was born, I AM!" <u>*Titus 3:5,*</u> Jesus saved us, not because of righteous things we have done, but by his mercy. Jesus saves us through the washing of rebirth and renewal by the Holy Spirit. (So, understand this, trying to be a GOOD PERSON does not get you into Heaven. That is Satan's lie to mankind. Just let your ego fueled by Satan tell yourself that you are such a good person. Good people get to go to heaven.)

The only unpardonable sin is to despise the gospel and deny the Holy Spirit) <u>*Matthew 12:31-32.*</u> The Holy Spirit power is given to man via receiving Christ Jesus as Savior. <u>*Roman's 10: 22-23 "Pure Righteousness,*</u> is given through faith in Christ to all who believe. There is no difference between Jew and Gentile for all have sinned and fallen short of the glory of God." (ahhh, we do not believe we are sinners because we do not murder, or steal! We are good!)

<u>*Romans 10:9*</u> *"The* salvation in Christ is a precious gift and it is nothing that can be earned through doing good works." <u>*Eph 2:8-9*</u> "for by grace, you, have been saved through FAITH. In addition, this is not your own doing; it is a gift from God, not a result of good works, so that no one may boost." (Satan wants you to believe that your good works will save you.)

***<u>*Roman's 3:23-24*</u> *"all* are justified freely by his grace through the redemption that came by Christ Jesus who was presented as a sacrifice of atonement, all must receive him by faith not by doing good works." {Yes, we desire to be good and do well unto others}

Romans 3:20_ " By trying to self-make yourself justified by being a so-called good person does not SAVE YOU"._Gal. 5:4"_ **By believing you can justify yourself; you are severed from Christ."** {Only Christ can change a bad consequence to a good or great consequence.}

***Romans 6:14-17 (New Intl. version)_ A Christian can still sin because sin is still your enemy but you are no longer a slave to sin. However, we will have consequences for our choices. Moreover, how we ask for forgiveness! If we do not ask for forgiveness, we will experience the consequence of our sin. When we ask for forgiveness through Christ salvation redemption; Christ payment for the sin circumvents the consequence of our sin. (Again, I say, "ONLY CHRIST CAN CHANGE A BAD CONSEQUENCE TO A GOOD OR GREAT CONSEQUENCE.")

Matthew 22: 37-40, "Love the Lord your God with all your passion, prayers, and intelligence. Also, love others as well as you love yourself." (In addition, do not hate yourself for the errors in your life, for God wants you to love yourself as He loves you)

Luke 23:34 Forgiveness is for all Christ said on the cross **_"Forgive them for they know not what they do!"_** _. (This statement was not just for the men who put him on this cross; this statement was for all of mankind for Christ knew the Nature's of the Flesh are given to us from Satan to destroy us and make us hurt ourselves and others.)_ ***For only by Christ salvation redemption can one overcome evil.**

***Proverb 8:8_ **"It is our duty to find the word of God, read it, and believe it to obtain its wisdom." We are a partner with God Almighty: so, make time to praise and trust in Christ salvation to gain supernatural divine wisdom, true fellowship, anointed worship, pure righteousness, and a real energy empowerment in The Holy Spirit. Amen, We have power in The Trinity.**

Read these scripture references' and seek new scriptures; ask God to guide you and daily you **will find revelation and power in His word. As you read these scriptures write down what God is expressing to you, as you are in an anointed state to live in Him revealing to you very important things for you and your family's life here on earth.**

What are your immediate daily needs? Seek what scriptures God has given mankind in His Bible to empower you, your family, your loved ones and your business, career, work plus all the recreations you want to enjoy. God wants to enhance every aspect of our life here on earth as it is in heaven. The smallest request of finding a parking spot close to the doorway of where you are going to also, stopping a fire coming close to your house. I have experienced success with both these examples because I asked for the Lord's help. Become a best friend to God Almighty our Father who art in heaven, Christ the word of creation, and the energy empowerment of the Spirit of Truth. "The Trinity" seeks to engage in fellowshipping daily with you, in His word God reveals how we become Christlike.

Chapter 3. "Jesus is Here Now in Us: He gives us forgiveness.

We are to forgive others while we are here on earth."

Heaven is real I have been lifted there four different times in my life. When in the heavenly presence we shed our earthly body. We have "our" complete identity; we recognize as our self, being so <u>Holy whole and totally complete in a supernatural divine love, joy, peace, and wisdom</u> not known in the earthy body in our flesh. Yet, it is enhanced and perpetual in our true image of being in Spirit: as <u>a spiritual Saint in Christ salvation living here on earth and within the heavenly realm. Be Love become the omnibenevolent character of the Trinity.</u> It is becoming who we are in the Holy Spirit anointing us here on earth as it is in heaven.

Matt. 6:9-13 The Lord's Prayer in chapter 10 reveals a depth to God's word.

<u>"We have in partial a true power from redemption salvation through Christ the word of creation, an Omnipotent, Omnipresent and Omniscient anointing when we choose to use his word. Isaiah 55:11 the word of the Lord will not return void unto him but shall accomplish all it is said to achieve, you will go out with joy and be led forth with peace.</u>

In Christ 2nd coming wherewith we gain fully all powers in Christ. Because we will no longer be fighting within our true spiritual being verses the natures of the flesh. Which now here on earth try to daily thwart our spiritual power in Christ.

Matt 16:19, "God gives us the keys to heaven: Whatsoever things we bind on earth will be bound in heaven and whatsoever things we choose to loosen from heaven will be loosed on earth. *Matt. 6:9-13* …. "On earth as it is in Heaven." This is a very clear instruction.

When we truly seek our Spirit being to lead us into Godly Options of choices for the day: we have magnificent glimpses of living within Christ and a Holy Spirit empowerment. We recognize when it is the flesh stimulating our emotions verse a Holy Spirit moment of joy, which has just conquered the natures of the flesh. Pure joy exists even when someone insults you!!! Being in that place at that moment in time is for the purpose of you being the one to pray for that person. We through being together are supposed to help each other fight off the natures of the flesh to overcome evil ideas and actions from Satan.

***One reason why humans are birthed into this earth is to show the light and love of Christ to others not as a religion but as true brethren in pure fellowship.

Forgive with a pure heart, the way Christ forgives us. God knows that Satan fuels the natures of the flesh, so he wants us to forgive others as he forgives us.

Luke 23:34 "Forgive them for they know not what they do." Never condemn the person again. Especially to other people because you want them to dislike the person who did you wrong. Our purposed is to pray for that person by placing Holy Hedge around them so as Satan can no longer fuel that weakness in their flesh. Which tries to bring out the bad natures in your flesh then you both become puppets to Satan's ideas: greed, vengeance, anger, hatred, gossip, to inflict emotional or physical injury to the other person. God warns us of the importance of pure forgiveness. God knows it is Satan enslaving a person to desire the vile natures in the flesh that destroys a person. The laws of the universe are God's ways to resolve evil. God does not do bad things to us; it is the consequences of our wrong choices.

Luke 6:37, "Do not judge, and you will not be judged. Do not condemn, and you will not be condemned. Forgive, and you will be forgiven."

Mark 11:25 "And when you stand praying, if you hold anything against anyone, forgive them, so that your Father in heaven may forgive you your sins."

Matt.6:13,15 If you forgive other people when they sin against you, your heavenly father will also forgive you. But if you do not forgive others their sins, your Heavenly father will not forgive your sins. (This means by your own choice you will experience the consequences of your sins. You will not lose your salvation, but you will pay the price for that sin. However, if you forgive another of their sins then your sin is extinguished.)

Matt 18: 21-23 Peter came to Jesus and asked "Lord, how many times shall I forgive my brother or sister who sins against me? Up to seven times?"

Jesus answered, "I tell you, not seven times, but seventy times seven!"

John 8:12 Again Jesus spoke to them saying 'I am the light of the world. Whoever, follows me will not walk in darkness, but will have the light of life.'

God created the laws of consequences upon creation. Once you receive Christ salvation you become His child once again and have defeated the curse of death. You have power over the natures of the flesh to stop Satan from fueling the natures of the flesh. Your transgressions are forgiven but you must forgive others just as Christ has forgiven you.

1st John 1:7-9 "It is God's will that we walk in the light as he himself is in the light, we have fellowship with one another and the blood of Jesus, His son, cleanses us from all sin. If we confess to Jesus our sins, He is faithful and righteous to forgive us of our sins and to cleanse us from all unrighteousness." You gain a real sense of pure Joy when you defeat the flesh.

Ephesians 6:14. Our loins are girded in truth. _1ˢᵗ Cor. 12:4-12_ Revelation, prophecy, wisdom, discernment, casting out evil, prayer language, interpretation of prayer language, healing and affecting miracles. _Psalms 32:8_ God instructs, teachers, and guides us.

1ˢᵗ Thes. 5:16 pray over everything never ceasing "Lord with me in this that I do."

Note: We cannot walk in the light of the Trinity if we believe in reincarnation (we are not and have never been old souls. That is Satan's lie to mankind; to make us believe we are less than an angel who became a demon. We are born once and have eternity in either Hell or Heaven. Yet, we do have the fellowship with our ancestors in the heavenlies through divine fellowship with Christ). We especially are never coming back as a dog or any other animal. All animals have an instinct to survive. Animals do not create new inventions and cannot read or write. Any animal's way of life is limited to the creatures God created each animal to be with certain defined characteristics.

Satan loves to bamboozle mankind into believing they are something they are not. Satan wants us to lose our powers in being created in God's image. We are above all creatures by being created in God's image which is truly being higher than the Angels: we are Saints by the Trinity being within us, who are redeemed through Christ salvation and have the power of God's word which is omniscient, omnipotent, omnipresent

Isaiah 55:11 God's word will not return void unto him, but will accomplish all it is purposed to achieve. You will go out with joy and be led forth with peace. We are purposed to learn what this means in being created in God's image. This desire in us will be perpetually evolving throughout eternity.

By LindaJane Chapman via a Holy Spirit anointing

Chapter 4 " God's Word in Us is Omnipresent, Omnipotent, and Omniscient!"

***HOLY everlasting in peace and completeness; as we are originally created in God's image and we, "HIS Saints" by HIS word; we become omnipresent, omnipotent, omniscient, omnibenevolent; within God's guidance always giving us Holy options to choose from daily.

The Omnipresent power of God is a true delight whenever we apply it to our life. Here is a fun story. I will give you a summary of the events that took place in achieving this adventure. In December 1999 God gave me a message to give to Kevin Costner. I know this sounds impossible but with God all things are possible! *Matt. 19:26, This story is proof*

After writing the message down and I called a friend, Jack Kelly, who goes to all the movie premieres in Hollywood. I planned to go to the premiere of "For Love of the Game" (This has a spiritual association that it was this movie at the time: Satan plays, his "games" of ruin daily with us while God gives us victory when we listen to him!)

While I was driving 2 ½ hours I started contemplating how I was going to meet Kevin to give him the letter with God's message: The Lord spoke to me telling me what to say first when I met Kevin before giving him the envelope. I thought 'what a crazy thing to say to someone! Ok Lord if you say so I will say it.' Laughing at how crazy, is this statement.

Well, several accidents on the freeways made me late and Jack was not there, I prayed, 'Lord Help me do this that you have assigned to me to do!' Standing by the check in table wondering 'How am I going to get in?' Sean Young, the actress who did the movie with Kevin in 1987, "No Way Out," greets me like I was a longtime friend, puts her arm around me, "How have you been?" and walks me into the theater, I think, 'wow that was powerful. I only met her once and just said Hello. How could she remember me? Thank You, Jesus. You did say ask and you will receive' *Luke 11:9-13* "For everyone who asks receives, the one who seeks finds, the one who knocks, the door will be opened."

I walked up to the first screening room I saw in this multiplex that had all screens showing the premiere this night. The girl at the entrance says in tough voice, "Where is your ticket?"

I answer, "My friend, Jack, is inside and he has my ticket!"

She replies, "well he will have to come back out and get you because I am not letting you in here without a ticket in your hand!"

I thought 'wow, help me Jesus help me now!' I walked up the stairs to the next screening room, where a tall blond girl was checking tickets explaining to her that my friend, Jack is inside with my ticket. She said "No I can't let you in."

Right then a bunch of people came up the stairs, the attendant had to check them in so, I motioned to the girl saying, "I am going in to find my friend OK!" She nodded yes. (ahh again God's perfect timing)

2 Peter 3:8 "God has perfect timing: never early, never late. God is never in a hurry, but he is always on time!" God blesses us with his scriptures to anoint our life.

The movie was truly great, sentimental, passionate and a message of love. I was born in Detroit and the Tigers always hold a special place in my heart. As the movie ended, my mind goes to 'now where can I find Jack?' the Lord tells me to "Exit now, now!" I leave scanning every area looking for Jack. Thinking 'God told me to exit. So maybe I will find Jack in the courtyard?'

Everyone entered at different times but exiting was likened to sardines stuffed in a can shoulder by shoulder inching out the doors one by one. This woman on my right shoulder starts talking to the man on my left shoulder as we were squeezed together trying to exit. She asked him, "Did you like the movie? Are you going to the party?"

He answers right before we are exiting the door, "yeah I liked the movie but don't like those after parties," he puts his ticket in his jacket upper breast pocket.

Then the Lord tells me to "ask him for his party ticket." My mind goes into a panic 'I can't do that; I can't do that!' I argue a few seconds with God, then as this man and I are still walking side by side up to the sidewalk, out of my mouth comes, "I liked the movie, but I lost my friends who have my party ticket! I can't find them!"

He looks at me with a big smile, "So you want to go to the party!" as he hands me the party ticket. I thanked him. Thinking 'Wow that was a miracle.'

Walking up to the tented area behind the Century Plaza Hotel I see the same girl who was nasty to me at the first screening room, she says to me "I guess you found your friends!"

A big smile graced my face as I replied, "Yes, I have friends in high places!"

Right then and there I thought, 'Thank you Jesus. When God gives you an assignment, He helps you through it and you know with no doubt that He took you there!' "If God brings you to it, He will bring you through it." This is not a bible scripture, but it is implied.

I entered the party: food and drink kiosks were placed around a secured area with security guards keeping people out of the extra special VIP section. Music was playing and everyone was having a great time. As I started to walk around the VIP area my eye caught John Travolta's eye, His wife Kelly Preston, was the star with Kevin Costner. I nodded to him as we had met several times through the years, but it had been 15 years since I last saw him. He told the security guard to let me in. It was like the parting of the red sea. I walked up to his table as he said to me "Out of everyone here I know, I know you." We chatted about our mutual friends. He introduced me to Kelly and the actor, Jay Mohr, then John asked me to sit down. I agreed, we took a photo of us all together.

Then I told him, "I want to go out and get a drink. I will come back." Looking at three empty tables and I wondered if those were Kevin's. As I returned there was Kevin Costner all alone standing by those tables. I thought 'when have I ever seen an actor after his movie stand all alone at his tables.' This was for sure a very rare incident. Kevin's back was towards me. I put down my drink and walked up behind him putting my hands gently on his shoulders whispering in his left ear, what the Lord told me to tell him. "If you would have been born in the 1700's you would have gone down in history as a great explorer."

He swooped around saying to me "You've got that right!" I introduced myself and told him I have a message for you from God and handed him the letter, telling him to read it later as it has an important message in it for you.

He said to me, "please stay here, I have to find my daughter, Lilly I will be right back. Stay here, stay here!"

While I was standing there a girl was chatting with one of the security guards asking if I was Linda Chapman. The guard asked me, and I said "yes", she let the girls into the VIP area right when Kevin came back. She was a friend from Brazil who I had not seen in 20 years. The crowd was a mob scene now and Kevin was having so many people coming up to him. I touched his forearm saying, "May I have a kodak moment?" as I handed the camera to my friend, and she took the picture.

I never did find Jack. But I knew God purposed me to know that it was him who did everything for me that day because I was obedient… it is so much fun to walk in the realm of heavenly things on earth. *Matt 6:10*. God entrusted me with his word for Kevin, *Isaiah 55:11* "So shall God's word go forth and not return void unto him but shall accomplish all He desires it to achieve. You will go out with joy and be led forth with peace". "I Love You Jesus" We are purposed to do God's work here on earth.

Yes, curiosity is a fundamental part of being creative and God bestowed a creative nature upon us. However, that was to be stimulated by our freewill choices in God's realm. Until Satan bamboozled Adam with a lie; that gave us "mankind," the natures of the flesh and eternal death in hell. Christ Jesus when we receive HIM gives us back eternal life in heaven and the ability to conquer the evil in ourselves, and mankind here on earth if we apply HIS word.

***The WORD is creation, and the WORD is the Son of God Almighty, who came to empower us daily to defeat the natures of the flesh: which only hinder our identity in first being created in God's image. We are in Christ truly redeemed, "The Word of Creation."

1st John 5:7 *** "for there are three that bear record in heaven, the Father, Christ the Word, and the Holy Spirit: and these three are one." {The Trinity}

Adam was 1st created in the image of God Almighty; birthed into *pure righteousness, divine wisdom, true fellowship, anointed worship and real power in the Holy Spirit* with God Almighty, "I AM". Adam traded that power and wisdom, for the knowledge of good and evil: which allows Satan to feed our flesh desires, which makes us feel good about doing bad things and we can justify those actions by the flesh being satisfied. Thus, the flesh has control over our desires and how we make our choices in life.

Yes, even what seems to be a great choice can even take us down a path of good things but that was not the perfect path GOD wanted us to choose from. Oh yes, we will still be blessed. However, there is that glimpse of Holy Spirit empowerment that comes when we make GODLY CHOICES IN OUR LIFE. We learn to know the difference and more and more start to experience those truly HOLY Pure experiences from being on the path God has ordained for our life. God Loves to move through us as his saints, his vessels here on earth, blessing our lives with all great things. Yet, whenever we make wrong choices, he leaves only to be preparing to guide us through the battle we put ourselves into.

. *1st John 3:8* God cannot tolerate sin, and that is why He sent His son "to destroy the devils works." Our wrong choices make us have bad experiences. Godly choices make great experiences. Only Christ can change a bad consequence to a great one.

Originally, the Body was only the container of the awesome empowerment of being created in God's image. The Trinity gave us our freewill choices in life. God gave mankind curiosity with the ability to create. Remember Adam had just named all the animals that GOD created for mankind to enjoy here on earth. There was tremendous power in making those choices for life. Adam realized he did not have a mate like the other animals. God wanted Adam to need a help mate; so, as he could take that part of Adam to create Women. *Genesis 1:28,* God's purpose for Adam and Eve was for them to "be fruitful and become many and fill the earth." We are made in God's image; we are to fill the earth with more Human beings than the angels God created. Satan can only work with the angels that followed aka Lucifer in the heavenly battle to overthrow God in heaven. We created in God's image are to reproduce more human beings in numbers here on earth than the angel/demons here on earth. We are fighting in the final battles as Saints in God's image to overthrow all evil in the earth.

Also, *Genesis 49:10* God wanted his nation of Judah, to populate so that they would not be oppressed by Satan fueling their enemies to destroy them. God purposed the tribe Judah to produce the Messiah, who would save all of mankind who believed in Christ salvation.

I believe that Eve was not in the garden *Gensis 2:18,19* when God told Adam not to eat of the tree of the knowledge of good and evil. *Gensis 3:4-6* Then when speaking to the woman Satan lied twisting God's word as Satan usually does do; that if you were to partake upon this tree of good & evil in the garden that GOD said, "do not eat of this tree or you will surely you will die" Satan enticed Eve to touch the fruit and nothing happened, so she saw it as good to gain knowledge. Satan told Eve, "Surely, you will not die." Adam and Eve did not know what "Die" meant! Plus, Adam was already made in God's image; he didn't need to know evil. But Satan wanted Adam and all mankind to suffer disobedience. Know this one thing in life, Satan wants what we have, to be made in the image of God and have God's powers. We in Christ salvation redemption gain back God's powers in us if we utilize God's word. *Genesis 22:14* The Lord will Provide "Jehovah Jireh" *Job12:13* to God belong wisdom and power; counsel and understanding are His.

Satan says, "You will be like gods, and you surely will not die" ***Adam made a choice out of the gifts from God: Curiosity and creative nature. Adam's Wrong choices created very bad consequences for mankind. Adam was disobedient: God knows all things "omniscient, omnipotent, omnipresent" and he set into motion upon creation the laws of consequences. ****If you make wrong choices, you get bad consequences, if you make right choices, you get good consequences, yet if you make Godly choices, you get great consequences. Again, I say remember Only Christ can change a bad consequence into a good or great consequence. The outcome depends on how we ask for forgiveness or for His help .*

God knows all things that does not mean he wants that to happen! Yet, The Trinity will always be there when we as redeemed in Christ salvation call out for his help.

Hey one more very important thing to practice is to pray for those who do not know Christ, so as they get through their bad choices with help from The Trinity. So as they will come to see how God Almighty has helped them even though they have not yet received Christ into their life. It is our purpose to pray for everyone friend or foe. This is how we redeemed in Christ stop Satan from enslaving people to do vile evil acts in this world we live in.. *John 3:17* God did not send Christ into the world to condemn the people but that all in the world would be saved.   Amen

Going back to the story of the Russian mafia man, Oleg , who threaten my life with a knife held to my face. God guided me on where to go in that house : whereas, his audience of his Russian Attorney, his new Body guard , his Russian interrupter , and his Russian wife were all standing there in the living room watching as he viciously threaten me. There is a lot more to this story that I will reveal at another time. But at this moment in time, I had to get out of the house. God told me what to say as I stepped away from the knife in his hand. With a smile on my face, I likened to a ditzy blonde, cocked my head and said softly, "ahh, I have to go upstairs and finish arranging the accessories that were just delivered!" Thinking to myself as I walked upstairs, 'Lord, get me out of here! give me the words to say Lord.'   I quickly put the sculptures into place. Then I heard steps coming up the stairs as Oleg walked into the room, I stared at him as I walked six feet next to him eye to eye shoulder to shoulder, I whispered in his ear with a stern soft eerie voice, "Don't push me to far!" walking passed him. Like Christ in the Garden of Gethsemane walked by the guards. I was so strong in my spirit I had absolutely no fear,

Yet Oleg ran getting ahead of me down the stairs screaming, "Get her out of here now!!"

 The bodyguard pushed the buttons opening the door and the outside gate. I walked out and got into my car, my hands and knees were shaking. I drove Serpentine, through dark alley ways with my lights out, making sure no one followed me. Then God told me, 'I took you upstairs so there were no witnesses to what My Holy Spirit in you was saying to Satan in Him. He has killed many people in front of others that is why they are so very afraid of him.'

I praised the Lord for keeping a smile on my face and not allowing Satan's fear nature to overcome me. Marty Goetz lyrics came alive for me "He is my defense I shall not be moved!" I had a supernatural strength beyond belief. I had NO fear until I left that house.

So many details are truly compelling in this experience, but I will have to share them another time. It is a long story with many twists and turns.

What is important here is that a week after this the Lord told me to write Oleg a letter. I told Oleg to receive Christ into his life to ask for forgiveness for all the killings and vile things he had done; that Christ would forgive him. Expressing to him that the gifts God gave him are better than the actions of evil he is doing. It was a long-detailed letter and I drove to another county to get a postmark from there just in case he might try to find out where I lived. I did not go back to the LA area for three months. In March I ventured back to Beverly Hills to see friends as I walked into "Maple Drive" restaurant, my friend, Jane was sitting at the bar. We chatted a few minutes and she said, "did you hear what happened to Oleg?"

I answered, "No, what happened?"

Jane informed me "He was in Russia, he opened his front door, and someone shot him; blowing his head off."

At that moment I knew why God purposed me to write him that letter. He probably had a few people praying for his salvation. I was the instrument to give him a final word. We are supposed to pray for all mankind, friend, or foe. God knows how the natures of the flesh Satan fuels to make us do crazy things. The Lord tells us to ask for His help and he is there to help guide us through all circumstances in our life. I know this is so very real because every time I asked the Lord for help, He is there for me. It is only through my own disobedience when I did not listen that I experienced a failure.

By LindaJane Chapman via a Holy Spirit anointing

Chapter 5 "The Nature's of The Flesh War Against Us, Who are Made in God's Image"

Again, I say God *knows all things, which does not mean he wants that to happen.* God gave mankind a freewill and many options to choose from. At that moment Adam ate of that forbidden tree, Satan birthed into mankind the desires of the natures of the flesh. Which in today's world Satan fuels daily to hinder our life in Christ here on earth.

***If God would ever go against HIS laws, HIS righteousness' will be destroyed. Therefore, He did not stop Lucifer from trying to coup d'état heaven; nor did HE stop Satan from tempting Adam with Lies! God allows consequence to be his resolve.

***We are God's workers here on earth and we are purposed to do His work here. Yes, we have *Mark 16:15-18* authority by Christ in us to cast out Satan and the evil natures of the flesh in others and ourselves. We are responsible for what happens here on earth. So do not blame God for your problems. God knows your wrong choices or another person's wrong choice in life is why you or a loved one may die earlier than God had planned.

God has never given little babies a death sentence by abortion. God never set that day for their death. Some people are cavalier and mislead thinking God knows when you will die as if that day is the only day you die. It is true God does know the day in advance, however, he knows that it is because of your bad choices or another person's wrong choice that hurt you. Maybe, you could have stopped it; if you were obedient to what God was telling you. Yet, that is not the date he planned for you to die, yes God did know that day was possible.

In 1973, The Lord told me 3 x 3 times to not get on a certain plane leaving Hawaii. I had missed my original flight because the wicky-wicky bus driver didn't stop at Pam Am. I just wanted to get on the next Pam Am flight...The Lord kept telling me, "Don't get on that TWA flight," I had a connecting flight to New York to do my decorating project, I was doing for Bobby Riggs, (The infamous tennis player who was really promoting women's tennis with Billy Jean King at the time with a grand play off. It was exciting for me to be a part of that passionate tennis enthusiasm!) I really did not want to go on that TWA flight to LAX because my spirit kept telling me "Do not get on that plane." But the supervisor forced me to take that flight! I was in an airplane accident whereas, I was injured, dead people crushing my body. This incident proves how if we let other people make our choices we can get into trouble. This is a long story revealing a healing 5 years after the accident and my lawsuit was finalized in 8 years, all the horrific, overwhelming details and then anointed miracles will be told in my auto biography.

Our choices or any other persons can create our problems or even death. From experience I say, "If you are old enough to know how to cast evil off a person you can save lives. '<u>Satan get off of this person NOW BY THE NAME AND BLOOD OF JESUS THE CHRIST.</u>' *<u>James 1:13</u> "God cannot be tempted by evil and He, Himself does not tempt anyone but each one is tempted when he is carried away by his own lust".*

So do not blame God for your problems. It is so important to never think that God wants to hurt you to give you a lesson. It is your choice's that puts you there. However, Christ will still come to your rescue! The purest love of all is the Omnibenevolence in The Trinity. The Old Testament battle actions by God through mankind bringing about God's laws of consequences are now extinguished through Christ salvation redemption: for everyone who chooses to enact Christ salvation authority in The Trinity. God does not harm us; God warns us and still battles for us when we make wrong choices. Be thankful and grateful for HIS help through the resolve of your mistakes in life.

Chapter 6 " Idolatry in Paganism was Before the Hebrews:

God's chosen people, ordained to have a pure undefiled bloodline. So as Christ, "The Word of Creation," could come giving mankind the option of a freewill choice for redeeming salvation.

God created a chosen people, (a new birthright creating the Hebrew nation.) *Gensis 12:1-3, Gen.15, & Gen 17:7,* **through Abraham's obedience a covenant was established .. Obedience is our key to being blessed by The Trinity. Do not second guess what God is telling you to do. Just obey what and when he tells you to do it.**

Being challenged with the future of my daughter, Chrystall, in December of 1988 was my own personal Abraham moment. Wow, one must take a deep breath when your spirit-being, and your mind are so strong in trust and faith, but your emotions and your physical body are feeling like a limp wet noodle. This is a very long-involved story about my wonderful marriage and how it happened to end in a divorce. I am only going to tell you all about my day in court, (as Paul Harvey would say) 'the rest of the story', will be in my auto-biography .. truly compelling and a little bit crazy but good crazy. I am very happy I married Michael! We did have fun.

Michael, my husband, started having some off the chart's behavior. So, my Mother In-law suggested we all do family counseling. We would all meet with her psychiatrist and then I would have a private 30-minute consultation with Dr. Geddes in Orange County. Also, where my father In-law had a big law firm. One day to my surprise I got divorce papers stating that Michael wanted full custody of Chrystall, she was 3 years old .. He apparently got another woman pregnant, and they were going to be a solid family unit for Chrystall after our divorce. Instead of Chrystall, being with me, her mother, who had an interior design business and would not be around as much. Oh, right good ole Dr, Geddes gave a report stating, Michael was healed by taking his bio-Polar medicine. Yet, I was delusional about what was best for my daughter: even though my design office was in my home, and I had a live-in nanny. Well, God did tell me to marry Michael and God did tell me exactly when I would get pregnant with Chrystall. Those experiences in my life are truly heartfelt fun stories. It all was divine by God and amazingly I had pure joy: I would not change a thing!

Now, Chantel the new woman in Michael's life looked like Bo Derek. She was 12 years older than Michael and she bought him a Rolls Royce. Of which he was always trying to get me to trade in my fully paid for 450 SL Mercedes {I had before our marriage} as a down payment on a Rolls Royce and I would not do that period. My father In-law was a big-time lawyer in the Orange County court system and knew most of the judges and attorneys who played golf with the judges, if you get my drift here… I was little David fighting Goliath.

I got down on my knees and prayed, 'Lord guide me through this, Help me Jesus! Give me supernatural wisdom' _Psalms 32:8_ "God instructs, teaches and guides us".

Phil 4: 13,19 "I can do all things through Christ who strengthens me. God will supply my every need." Internally crying out in thought 'I trust in you Lord; I trust in you to protect my daughter. Tell me what to do Lord!'

The Lord spoke to me "Do not say anything bad about Michael even if it is the truth!" Wow he had done so many crazy things that made me totally afraid of him taking Chrystall and doing something that could unintentionally harm her.

Yet, I had to trust in the Lord because this was his answer to my prayers. I told my mother, my attorney, and Chrystall's God-mother, Donna Messer.. Everyone repeatedly said the same thing to me, "you will lose your daughter if you don't tell what he has done. Linda it is the truth just say the truth!!!"

Mulling over in my mind the what if's. I never question the Lord as to why I should not tell the truth I just knew in my heart of hearts I had to obey what Christ told me.

It was my day in court. I called Donna, with non-stop weeping tears rolling down my face. "Please, come and be with me I can't drive the car. I am shaking. I am spiritually and mentally strong, yet I am emotionally and physically a wet noodle. I must meet my attorney at the courthouse!"

As she drove me, I started to pray out loud, "Lord Chrystall is your child first and foremost Lord, you will protect her. I trust you, Lord. I lay her on your alter Lord God Almighty just like Abraham laid Isaac, I trust in you to care for her all the days of her life. I pray Michael will realize how he could unintentionally harm her by his careless acts. It is his ego that wants her. Lord rise every ounce of Love he has for her and make him realize how he could hurt her. Pierce His Heart Lord that he loves her more than his ego. Lord let him realize why he needs a conservator for his visitations. I place Chrystall in your hands Lord, I trust in You. She is your child first. I am not asking for child support or alimony Lord; you will take care of both of us. I trust you, Lord, to take care of Chrystall all the days of her life."

We got into the courtroom. I sat there praying "75,000 angels fill this room now! Lord please, give me peace of mind, spirit, and emotions. Lord, give me wisdom on what to say."

The judge entered and our case was called. The judge looked at me with contempt and a snarky voice said, "What makes you think Mr. Friedemann can't be alone with his child?"

I gasp as my mind was racing, I took a deep breath, remembering what the Lord had told me, "Do not say anything bad about Michael even if it the truth!" I put my finger up signaling as I swallowed taking a breath while praying 'Lord, tell me what to say', suddenly out of my mouth with a sweet soft whisper, "Michael why don't you tell the judge."

Michael went on and on telling the judge how he flew a car over a building site like Evel Knievel and they had to get a crane to pull the car out, He told them of the time he ran his Rolls Royce through a wall at a bar. Then he confessed to going to Mexican airlines half dressed, no long pants on in a speedo bathing suit, a Brooks Brothers pin stripped jacket with a tie and no shirt on, while he was asking for free passage because he was a missionary. He then told the judge that the airline's called the police, and he went to jail for disorderly conduct at Mexican airline that day.

The most unique thing happened when he grabbed his chest and said with tears in his eyes, "I feel like my heart is being pierced, I love Chrystall so much, I love her so much I could accidentally hurt her. It is my ego that wants her. Linda should be the conservator. Linda will always be fair and know when I can visit Chrystall. Linda should be the conservator."

The judge immediately said, "we will take a break get with your attorney's and come back in an hour."

I was in awe of God when those words that I prayed came out of Michaels mouth. I stayed quiet and kept praying, "Lord please don't let them change his mind, Lord I will be fair with Michael any time he wants to visit with Chrystall. I am not asking for alimony or child support. You will take care of Chrystall, Lord she is your child first and foremost. You will take care of both of us. I praise you Lord Jesus, *Psalms 118:24* for 'this is the day the Lord has made. I will rejoice and be glad in it!' *Matt. 19:26.* "With man this is impossible, but with God all things are possible."

Isaiah 14:24 " *As I have planned, so shall it be, and as I have purposed, so shall it stand.* We came back into the court room and Michael repeated what he said early in the court, so it was order as such that day. I got to keep Chrystall, and I was the conservator for visitations.

This was my Abraham moment as I laid Chrystall on that altar I knew in my heart the Lord would protect her all the days of her life. Later I found out that judges were giving custody of the children to men. Stating that the women were mean spirited out of jealousy of another woman being with their husbands before the divorce. If a woman said anything bad about the husband, she was surely going to lose in court. God knew that and God prepared me.

The story of Abraham's faith has always had a great impact on my life. Often, I have prayed that I would have the faith and trust to do exactly what God told me to do with confidence. This time it was really put to the test. We all need to aspire to have a great faith and trust in what God tells us. _Proverbs 3:5,6_ Trust in the Lord with all your heart and lean not unto your own understanding but in all your ways acknowledge God and He will direct your path.

It took a very long time before God found a person like Abram on earth, who would truly listen to him, trust in him and be obedient to what he told him to do.

God had to keep this bloodline pure to be able to birth His Son, "The Word of Creation", into earth to achieve the salvation for God's children. We are created in God's image, and we must truly desired salvation to become renewed and sanctified.

After the knowledge of the covenant with Abraham in The Old Testament, we find many other religions through Idolatry that were created before the Hebrew nation is created. They are the "Pagan" religions made by Satan to worship everything of the earth, sea, and sky. Making idol worship to control mankind with Satan's false ideas. In a sense, humans worship Satan without knowing they are. Because the nature of the flesh in Idolatry is being satisfied through worshipping idols. Satan makes up things while God creates things.

The first sin of Lucifer in heaven was covetous idolatry and the first sin of Adam was idolatry."You will be like God." Adam already was created like God, yet Satan fooled him.

Many times, we see in the Bible whereas the Hebrews were being persecuted. The battles the Hebrews had to fight to keep their bloodline pure were tremendous. They were fighting numerous pagan religions. Satan was empowering them to destroy the Hebrews to enslave them. Remember, upon Satan seducing Adam into disobedience was Mankind's fall from God's grace. God told Satan "The seed from the woman will bruise His heel while Crushing your head, Satan"! Satan does everything to hinder that happening.

Satan fueled hatred in the Pagan religions to go against the Hebrews. The Jewish people have been persecuted longer than any other culture or religion in the world.

Wars broke out among these Pagans and the Hebrews. This made a bad consequence for any other tribe going against the Hebrews. There were mass killings of men, women, and children in these Pagan religions, who were trying to kill the Hebrews. These religions were also sacrificing their own babies and children to the pagan God's. Satan wants to kill mankind, but Satan can't unless man agrees with envy, jealousy, hatred, greed, covetousness, murder, sexual perversions, all these bad habits create illnesses and idolatry. The Lord God Almighty had to keep the Hebrew bloodline pure to send Christ to earth. Those other cultures were under the influence of Satan's evil ideas to hurt the Hebrews. It is only by the blood of Christ that each person can conquer the evil natures of the flesh. Not until Christ came to earth, could this final forgiveness of sin be achieved. Now all people from every culture can receive Christ forgiveness. Christ Blood is pure. _John 3:17_ _"God did not send Jesus into the world to condemn the world but that all might be saved."_

There will always be the universal laws of God's consequences for choosing to go against what is best for mankind's salvation. It is a freewill choice! Again, I say, Satan birthed evil into humanity through Adam's disobedience. _James 1:13-14_ "Let no man say, when he is tempted that he is tempted by God, for God cannot be tempted by evil, and he, himself does not tempt anyone. Each one is tempted when he is carried away by his own lust." I repeat this utterance, God does not do any evil to us; it happens because of our choices or lack of not using God's power in us in stopping others who have chosen evil ideas. God's character is Omnibenevolent love. God will take a bad situation and give you blessings.

The body of man was to be a divine covering of the Holy Spirit. Then Satan seduced Adam. The flesh became the master of the body, making choices that became fueled by the natures of the flesh being in control and thus seeking satisfaction. ***This is why God tells us to die to the (natures of the) flesh is to gain in Christ. *** _Phil 1:21_ The only way to gain in Christ is through the word of creation to become empowered by the Holy Spirit in us, we utilize God's power in HIS omnipotent, omnipresent, and omniscient energy. Because _we are originally created in God's image. But Adam gave that power away through disobedience. God's word has tremendous power and is present when we speak it. God's Word goes everywhere he intends it to go._ _Isaiah 54:11._ "God's word will not return void unto him." _John1:1_ "In the beginning was the word and the word was with God and was God." **The WORD of Creation is Christ, the son of God . In Christ we gain back divine power.**

Jesus told us _John 14:12-30_ that when he left, he was sending one "The Holy Spirit" whereas we would do greater things than he did. We as Christians have not stepped up to our inheritance in Christ Power yet. Oh, somewhere someone said, "all that spiritual stuff is of the devil." Well, it is not. It is truly our power over the devil. _We need to learn to obey God's word_: Trust in what God is saying through His scriptures.

***To own our identity in Christ. Learn what natures of the flesh are hindering our empowerment in Christ and cast them out daily especially, off our family, friends, loved ones, their loved ones including ourselves and even onto any enemies.

If you do not have a pure Holy Spirit Anointing, evil can seduce you daily in the simplest options given to mankind via our choices!!

It is just that simple... We gain in partial many definite powers by Christ word. It is being divinely sent to us by God being Omnipotent, Omniscient, Omnipresent and Omnibenevolent. These Powers are magnified in CHRIST second coming, where we gain in whole these powers of being created in God's image; However, now we are in Christ omnipresent, omniscient, omnipotent and omnibenevolent in making freewill choices to build our life in being ORIGINALLY created in God's image with *Divine wisdom, true fellowship, anointed worship, pure righteousness and a real Holy Spirit energy empowerment authority over all evil. The best will come when we learn to utilize calling out our blessings!*

Now in Christ in us, we can utilize tremendous power in the Holy Spirit being in us whenever, we choose to use it. Yes, Omnipotent, Omnipresent, and Omniscient in His Word and Omnibenevolent in His character when we here on earth choose to defeat the vile natures of the flesh in ourselves and in others by utilizing the power given in us through The Trinity. A few Christians have verbally attacked me for saying this, however, remember the devil does not ever want you to tap into Christ's empowerment in you.

This action of utilizing God's word in me, as the Temple of The Holy Spirit, has saved me many times from being harmed by escaping many treacherous acts of evil by other people.

It is only by Satan's ideas that a person does not love the creator. It is a necessity to fellowship, praise, worship, trust, be obedient, and being grateful with a thankful heart that we can own our identity in receiving Christ salvation. I repeat: We gain the empowerment of the Holy Spirit. We become through using God's word; Omnipresent, Omnipotent, Omniscient, and Omnibenevolent when we ask the Trinity for help in any of the circumstance in our life. *1st thes 5:16* Pray over everything never ceasing. "Lord be with me in this that I do, *Psalms 32:8* Lord instruct, teach, and guide me." However, we must believe this and trust in God.(God wants you to love yourself as he loves you;)

****Luke 23:34* Forgiveness is for all. Christ said on the cross, "Forgive them for they know not what they do." The Trinity knows how Satan fuels the natures of the flesh and how we have a Godly power over these natures to cast them out of ourselves and others if we choose to use Christ word, and the Holy Spirit empowerment.

Satan must thwart all our desires to seek Godly choices. Satan fuels the flesh by physical touch, taste, sight, hearing, so the human body reacts in an instant and is diverted to the fascination in the world which blocks our spiritual awareness.

Oh, how people think they are so spiritual when it is truly only their flesh being satisfied. They get a little lift and a slightly high intangible feeling. Satan perverts a part of the God given gifts in our need to seek a spiritual life. Thus, creating a false spiritual sense in a new age movement thinking in a mystical way; instead of a Godly way of living a life *John 14:12-30* doing greater things than Christ did here on earth. No person could ever comprehend this power until Christ came to earth, died, rose again, went to the Father to send the Holy Spirit of Truth to give those who believe in Christ, the energy empowerment, and wonderment of the ethereal celestial energy of The Trinity. To have this life we must do more than just go to church randomly on holidays or every Sunday.

If you do not daily feed your spirit being more spiritual food for thought, then how will you ever know what God is telling you. Learn to spend time with The Trinity to Love God, the Father, Christ our Savior, and dwell in the empowerment of The Holy Spirit energy. Exercise *1st cor. 12:4-12* "revelation, prophesy, wisdom, discernment, casting out evil, prayer language, interpretation of prayer language, healing, and effecting of miracles." These are the gifts of the spirit. Do not be enticed by idolatry in Pagen religions that Satan fuels in mankind to stop you from learning who you are created to become in being made in the image of God. You are recreated through Christ salvation redemption to gain the real power in the Holy Spirit energy anointing your life.

Ask yourself, 'Why do I want to seek things that have a source from Satan's ideas?'

Probably because Satan lied to you about it being OK, you can do it! It won't hurt you! It doesn't matter. Hey that is exactly how Satan got Eve to touch the Tree and then go to Adam reporting, it's ok. It will give us knowledge!

Christian's wonder. 'Why am I having so many difficulties in life, and struggles even in the simplest tasks of the day? Hit and miss in blessings! What are my motivations in making one choice over another?' We ask the questions, but do we wait for the answer?

Whenever you make excuses as to why you have a right to do something your way: count on that choice sometime, somehow, someway compromising your life in other unimaginable ways. Why do you lust after putting yourself in Satan's battleground; just because everyone else is saying it's ok?

Is it rebellion and my ego wanting to defend my right in my flesh to do certain things my way. 'Oh, Ego how you fool me!' Do I truly try taking everything to The Trinity then wait for the Holy Spirit to guide me? Am I patiently looking for what God is telling me? Wrong choices put me into Satan's battleground where The Trinity will help me in the battle when I ask for forgiveness or for help. When all along if I made Godly choices, I would be in God's playground of abundant blessings where Satan cannot come to harm me. _Eph 6:16_ the shield of faith stops all the fiery darts of the enemy.

The new age movement in our society is Satan's tool to take God's word and pervert it .. Just as Satan did to Eve and Adam in the Garden of Eden. The lie was evident they were already like GOD almighty and did not need to know evil. **_Revelation 12:4_** remember Lucifer convinced 1/3 of the host of angels to follow Lucifer in an attempt to rule in heaven. Before Lucifer's fall from Grace **_Ezekiel 28:13_** Lucifer was known as the "son of the morning and called the anointed guardian cherub. Also sited in _Isaiah 14:12_. Trust in God's sovereignty, leave God's laws to resolve disobedience, and guard your heart against the sin of PRIDE.

Everything that the new age movement promotes is taken from the word of God in the scriptures, but the new age movement leaves out the need to honor God Almighty and the Son; (_john 1:1-3_) Christ the word of creation, who gives us back the powers in our relationship with the Trinity. But the new agers embrace all false religions and a false stimulate calling it the Holy Spirit; when that feeling they promote is only feeding the flesh not really giving anyone a true and pure Holy Spirit spiritual self-control but truly giving the opposite an enslavement to the **_flesh ruling the body instead of just being a covering of the Holy Spirit in the Trinity._**

Phil 1:21 When we die to the flesh rebuking Satan's vile ideas then we gain in Christ: a divine supernatural wisdom, true fellowship, anointed worship, pure righteousness, and a real energy empowerment in the Holy Spirit authority over all things. Amen PTL. Anything else we pursue is a lie from Satan to get you to feel good about doing bad things that you think are good; so, as you continue to commit Idolatry, the one sin that takes you to Hell for eternity with Satan. Because Satan hates the fact that mankind gets redemption from their disobediences and angels do not. **_Col. 2:8_** see to it that no man takes you captive by philosophy, and empty deceit, according to ' human traditions" or elemental demons and evil spirits of the world and NOT ACCORDING TO CHRIST EMPOWERMENT IN THE HOLY SPIRIT OF TRUTH. **_John 14:17_** the People of the world will not know the Holy Spirit of truth; because they neither see Him nor know him ; for He only dwells with those who receive Him as then He will be in you. To live in the spiritual realm of being created in God's image you must receive Christ salvation redemption.

Chapter 7 " Healing Scriptures" by Linda Chapman PrayerCoachUSA.com

I pray _Eph 6:16_, "Above all taking the shield of faith where with we will be able to extinguish all the fiery darts of the wicked". Now place a Holy Spirit hedge likened to _Job 1:8-10_ "a blessing and a protection hedge from God Almighty around _____, so as Satan cannot fuel any nature of the flesh in _____ (me/ them) to cause destruction of ____, (my/their) human body. I pray for complete healing inside each organ and tissues in_____ body. Holy Angels purify the air, foods, water, fluids; herbs, vitamins, minerals, medicine; body creams, lotions, hair and body products; paper goods, cleaning supplies, and all electronic machines plus the energy that is inside and around _____, externally and internally. Holy Angels purify everything around us and everything inside of us, as we are Christ Saints here on earth. Restore each cell in our bodies to Christ perfection with great health and well-being. All bad cells are commanded to flee immediately .. The laminin cross cell is commanded to be the energy of Christ in us and every cell in our bodies must renew to Christ perfection of health and well-being. The laminins are vital to biological activity, influencing cell differentiation, migration and adhesion. Christ is the authority in creation. I know that Christ in us is omnipresent, omnipotent, omniscient and can change the biochemistry of our bodies. We are re-created renewed in Christ and all bad cells are commanded to flee in Jesus' name we call forth the power of the Holy Spirit energy.

1st Cor.12:4-12. We Pray the empowerment of God's "revelations, prophesy, wisdom, discernment, casting out evil, prayer language, interpretation of prayer language, healing and effecting of miracles." Trust these gifts. _Matt. 8:13._ We agree for as it is done as you believe: we trust a complete healing inside each organ, all tissues and every cell in our body must renew to Christ perfection of health and well-being.

Phil. 4:8, I pray that, _____and all loved ones will, "only dwell on the lovely, pure, right, just, and the good report": The A+ for what we need to happen. Christ's Virtue will purify _____ life. May the good passions within our heart, thoughts within our mind, and words within our actions only dwell on these Holy Spirit anointed ideas.

Proverbs 18:20,21 "the tongue can make life or death!" {So be very careful what you say about yourself or your loved one}. Say "_____ has won the battle over the _____ illness attack. Lord, Bless and Guide us all in the foods, and fluids we choose to eat. Get the YUKA app. Do not buy any product that is below 50/100; seek the items that rate higher.

Matt.18:19,20. "for where two or more agree and are gathered in Jesus' name, The Trinity is with us all." Healing is real in today's world: trust in God's word, believe.

James 5:13-15 Live within, The Prayer of Faith. "Is anyone among you in trouble? Let him pray. Is anyone happy? Let them sing songs of praise. Is anyone among you sick? Let them call the elders of the church to pray over and anoint them with oil in the name of the Lord Jesus Christ. And the prayer offered in faith will make the sick person well, the Lord will raise them up. If they have sin, they will be forgiven. _Isaiah 54:17_ "No weapon formed against us will ever prosper" _Mark 16:18_ "We can pick up any poisonous thing and it will not harm us"

We all agree in prayer that _Psalms 32:8_ "God Almighty instructs, teaches and guides," the doctors, nurses, technicians, anesthesiologist, caregivers, nutritionist, and physical therapist etc. who assist in _____ complete healing process. _Phil.4:13_ "_____ can do all things through Christ who strengthens me/us/ them." Amen

Phil 4:19 "God Almighty will supply our every need," Physically, Spiritually, Mentally, Emotionally, Chemically, Electrically and Financially amen. We love you Jesus.

Amen. Five years after my airplane accident I was at "Church on the Way" at the 6 PM service. There was a guest speaker, he stood before us saying, "I had a whole other message for tonight: but the Lord just told me, 'There's people here who need healing.' So, anyone who needs a healing standup now as we say this prayer, receive your healing now!"

A lot of scriptures were being said, and the hum of people speaking in their prayer language filled the room. People were reaching their hands out toward all who were standing. I quickly stood up leaning on the chair in front of me, feeling a whirlwind of warmth flood my body from the top of my head to the tips of my fingers and toes. Ahh, raising up a coolness blew through my body, a tingling residue lingered with a pulsing vibration. I felt a healing energy fill my being and all my pain was gone from neck, back, knee and arms plus my back straightened. An indescribable joy lit inside me. I felt radiance. My friend, Starr Simpson was sitting down next to me, I touched her shoulder as she stood up to hold me it was like I was going to fall; only I wasn't falling I was soaring. She looked stunned at me as I softly said, "Starr I think the Lord just healed me!!"

Starr replied, "Now Linda don't get over groovy. We have been through this before!"

I gazed at her saying, "This is real. I feel renewed." My thoughts rushed 'Nothing is going to rob me of my healing; I know it is real this time!'

God's healing power is real in today's world even if you don't get it the first time you ask. Four months before I was at another religious convention it was televised and I stood up on TV, threw my cane away confessing a healing. I did feel adrenalin that subsided my pain but by the time I got to car my brother had to help me walk. The next day we went out to buy a cane. Once again, I say I will save the rest of the significate details for my autobiography. Five years of steadfastness, help, betrayal, and the exhaustion I lived through is for another time in sharing many other lessons learned during 1973 accident to the healing in 1978 and the lawsuit finalized in 1981.

Throughout my lifetime I have truly received numerous healings from people praying The Lord's scriptures over me. Dyan Cannon prayed for a healing of my shoulder: where I could not raise my arm for 8 months, and through my healing the doctors were stopped from operating on it. I have had several healings on my back, neck, teeth, arms, wrists, foot, knees, whereas the injured parts of my body were in excruciating pain for months and even years, then through prayers I gained a healing. However, several times I have had health issues that were not healed, and several people prayed over me and still I have no healing. Yet whenever I go through an episode and people cross my path to help me, we end up sharing the Lord and later they tell how it blessed their life. So, I do believe in healing I have had so many and yet not all, but God uses that to bring his people together for a purpose. The issues I have not been healed of are not life threatening either.

Ephesians 4:4 there is one body and one spirit, just as you were called to one hope when you were called, one Lord, one faith, one baptism; one God and father of all, and through all and in all who received him. _Ephesians 4:11_ so Christ himself gave to the apostles, the prophets, the evangelist, the pastors and teachers, to equip his people for works of service; so that the body of Christ may be built up until we all reach unity in the faith and in the knowledge of the son of God and become mature attaining to the whole measure of the fullness of Christ. _Ephesians 4:14-16_ We are no longer infants being thrown by the waves,.. We cast out cunning deceitful schemes. We speak truth in love, we grow to become every aspect of a mature body in Christ, who is the head and from him the whole body, joined and held together by every supporting ligament, tendons, tissue, bone, and flesh. We grow up in love in Christ as each part does its work. Trust in Christ Healing: Laminin is a cross.

By LindaJane Chapman via a Holy Spirit anointing

Chapter 8 "Scriptures to Heal Us All from the Loss of a Loved One"

I pray Christ supernatural divine strength, peace, comfort and eternal blessings to clothe all of our family and our loved ones through this tremendous loss of our beloved one. We are spiritual beings and have an eternity of life evermore in supernatural divine Love, Joy, and Peace. *2nd Corinthians 1:3-4* Blessed be the Father God of our Lord Jesus Christ the father of mercies and God of all compassion who comforts us in all of our afflictions.

Yes physically, emotionally, and mentally, we miss our time being with our loved ones. We pray that each reflection of good times shared brings each of us joy and love in each reminiscence. Love is a very powerful energy of delight, joy, passion, and caring for a person's wellbeing; these forces are alive with faith in Christ salvation redemption, we become Saints eternally living forever in a heavenly paradise. *Psalms 116:15* " *Precious in the sight of the Lord is the death of his beloved saints in Christ*" Once a person experiences the heavenlies, they realize the power of being purely righteous with no flesh natures hindering who we are created to be "Made In The Image Of God" *2nd Cor. 5:8,* "*We are confident, I say, and would prefer to be away from the body and at home with the Lord*" (Be happy for our loved one) Yes, we miss them and the time we share together! Know this we have life eternally.

John 22: 16 " *So with us and you: Now is your time of grief, but I will see you again and you will rejoice, and no one will take away your joy.*" *Joshua 1:9* " *Be strong and of good courage; be not afraid, neither be dismayed, for the Lord is with you wherever you go.*"

Phil 4:13 "*we can do all things through Christ who strengthens us.*" We must choose to rebuke the natures of the flesh that Satan fuels to defeat us with despair, worry, fear, anxiety, helplessness, anger, self-pity, and anguish. *Psalms 34:18* "Christ gives peace to the brokenhearted and saves the crushed spirit". *Matt 5:4* "*Blessed are they that mourn; for they shall be comforted.*"

Satan and the evil forces of the world want to fuel the natures of the flesh with suffering. Satan works daily to manifest pain emotionally, mentally, and physically. Christ said to Peter. *Matt 16:23* "Get behind me Satan, you do not have the concerns of God but merely concerns of the world." *Phil 4:19* "God supplies our every need supernaturally; spiritually, emotionally, mentally, chemically, electrically, physically and even financially etc." All prayers and scriptures ever given will feed your Loved one's spirit to choose Christ salvation in a split second. That Mustard seed of faith given to each person upon conception that has been hindered by the natures of the flesh will soar in a pure reality that they are made in the image of God. *John 3:17* "God did not send Christ into the world to condemn man but that all may be saved." *Luke 23:34* Christ said on the cross, "forgive them for they know not what they do" God knows the heart of every person and God knows how Satan has bamboozled them. God prefers that a person spends their whole life on earth in fellowship with The Trinity. Yet, God knows the heart of a person and knows other people's prayers for that person. The Lord knows the empowerment of HIS word and once the natures of the flesh can no longer hinder that person's awareness of accepting Christ forgiveness. Because they are truly made in the image of God Almighty; their spirit in a split second can receive Christ salvation redemption. Know that the word of God in Prayers is the most powerful life force in the universe. *1ˢᵗ thes 5:16* this is why we are purposed to pray over everything never ceasing. *Isaiah 55:11 "God's word will not return void unto Him but will accomplish all that is purpose to achieve you will go out with joy and be led forth with Peace."*

1ˢᵗ Cor. 15:42-44 "So will it be with the resurrection of the dead. The body that is sown is perishable; it is raised imperishable; it is sown in dishonor, it is raised in Glory; it is sown in weakness, it is raised in power; and it is sown a natural body, it is raised a spiritual body. If there is a natural body, there is a spiritual body." It is our choice Heaven or Hell! It is eternity. Every seed of scripture spoken over a loved one will manifest in their spirit life to choose Christ redemption. There is a life force in the word of God that soars in each person's spirit being when the flesh can no longer hinder choice. John 3:17 **God did not send Christ into the world to condemn people but that all would be saved through grace**. Once when I had walked away from God and felt very dead inside my spirit, I cried out to God to give me a sign. He lifted me to the heavenlies, I could see my body was face down in the sand. Yet I was above my body in the most vibrant place. I knew then that God gives a chance for you to receive Him when your spirit has left your flesh. The most important thing we can do is pray for our loved ones to receive him. *Act 16:31* Believe in the Lord Jesus, and you will be saved, you and your household.

2ⁿᵈ Cor. 1:3-4. "Praise be to God, the Father of compassion, who comforts all in their troubles, so that we can comfort those in trouble with the same comfort we received from Christ." Amen Try to remember it is Satan's natures of the flesh that create misery, pain, suffering whenever we lose a loved one. Now I am not saying you should avoid grief. However, it is good to cry and truly express heartfelt love for our loved one going forward, which is all a healthy natural process. Yet we must never allow Satan to enslave us be in torment over the physical loss of our loved one. That kind of pain Satan uses to hurt our physical body and causes illness. However, The Lord tells us in *psalms 116:15* "Precious in the sight of the Lord is the death of His Saints. He rejoices when they arrive at the gates of death, God welcomes those who love him."

Everyone reacts in different ways after the loss of a loved one. Also, it depends on what your responsibilities were with a person who passed on to Glory land. Do not be surprised if you find yourself avoiding things you did for them or together with them. Also, you may find that you start doing things you didn't do before but now are doing because they did it.

Three of the most impactful, emotional, and poignant experiences I have ever had were when My father died in 1999, My Mother died in 2013, and my Husband died in 2016 because I was assisting each with their healthcare needs and was there when they died. Three compelling inspirational stories but now I will only tell you of my reactions of after their passing away.

For two years, I would make a smoothie for my father when I would make my vitamin drink, The day he died I went into the kitchen looked at the blender and I could not raise my hand to grab it. I couldn't make a blended drink for 18 months. Then finally one day I could!

Every Christmas my mother wanted a new pair of pajamas. I would look high and low in every store, and I could never find the ones she wanted: no designer made them. She would get whatever I could find; but she wanted a certain color, size, and style. 18 months after her death I was shopping at Christmas time reminiscing me looking for her PJ's, and right on the rack was Ann Klein pajamas the color was pale pink and gray, the collar style and shape was perfect, two pockets at the bottom, and longer length on the pants. I looked up at the heavenlies laughing saying out loud, "Mama, I guess you told those clothing companies how to design the perfect style of pajamas! Here they are!" I bought them, now before this I never wore Pajamas, I love nightgowns, but when I got home, I put them on and now I wear Pajamas. I also wear my mother and father's shirts, jackets, and my dad's hats. I just feel like they are hugging me.

When my beloved husband, Col. Thomas M. Henry, passed on to glory, the next morning I went into the kitchen to make my breakfast, I couldn't get the pan out of the cupboard to fry an egg. Standing there frozen in time thinking, 'I am a gourmet chef; I love to cook. What's going on with me?' We had so many dinner parties where I would prepare the whole meal from appetizers, soup, salad, entrée, and desserts. Sometimes for 10 to 20 people for an elegant sit-down dinner. After Tom died it was 20 months before I could cook anything. Traveling made it easier for me. Then one day I was a house guest at Terry Moore's home in Santa Monica, she said how she likes fish. Out of my mouth came, "I will cook you an orange-roughy fish dinner tonight. It's one of my specialties'!"

After dinner Terry expressed praise saying," that is the best fish I have ever had in my whole life even when I was married to Howard, and we went to the best restaurants all over the world. Linda this was the best fish ever!"

Realize God will give you a blessing though your mourning .. Keep praying and know The Trinity is guiding you, comforting you and loving you through all things *Romans 8:28*, Praise the Lord. *Isaiah 41:13* For I am the Lord your God who takes hold of your right hand and says to you, do not fear; I will help you.

By LindaJane Chapman via a Holy Spirit anointing

Chapter 9 "Being Religious gives Us the knowledge of Christ.

Being in a Relationship with Christ gives Us a Holy Spirit Empowerment."

An example of having a relationship with The Trinity verse just knowing about Christ. _Matt 28:19_; God the Father, maker of Ideas; Christ the word of creation, the son of God, "I AM," The Savior, and the energy empowerment of the Spirit of Truth, The Holy Spirit, who God sent to live inside us as Christ has redeemed us so we work within the gifts of the spirit and the fruits of the spirit.

Just going to church on Sunday to satisfy the ritual of going to church to say you are a Christian but during the week you have no concern of Christ working in your life is truly likened to only knowing about Christ.

Matt 23:13-22, 27-28 "Woe unto you, scribes and Pharisees, hypocrites! For you are like unto whited sepulchers, (a monument of stone) which indeed appear beautiful outwardly, but within are dead men's bones. And of all uncleanness. Even so you also outwardly appear righteous unto men, but within you are full of hypocrisy and iniquity." They did not practice what they preached. _Matt 7:5-6._ Warning about hypocrites: "One who attacks others for their small flaws while ignoring their own massive ones, those who judge others but do not evaluate themselves". _Matt 7:13-23_ "Some will say 'Lord, Lord did not I do this_____, in your name….. The Lord answers, ' I never knew you. Away from me, you evil doers.' you cannot fake your way into the kingdom of God". _Hebrews 4:12_, "God's word is alive and active. Sharper than a two-edged sword, it divides soul and spirit; it judges the thoughts and attitudes of the heart." God knows where you lust after things of the flesh and where your heart is at all times.

Saying we are a Christian yet not seeking the empowerment of Christ sending the Holy Spirit of truth to guide us in our daily choices is not allowing our divine relationship in Christ in us to develop. We gain in the anointing by fellowshipping, praising, worshipping, learning the ways of the spirit in us and trusting the Lord's word.

Now here on earth God gives us the _gifts of the spirit_ to enhance our life. _1st Cor 12:4-12_, "revelation, prophecy, wisdom, discernment, casting out evil, prayer language, interpretation of prayer language, healing, and effecting of miracles." We can utilize these gifts if we explore them and allow the Holy Spirit to manifest within our request to God. We can be proficient in them. As we need to use each one with different degrees at different times for our family, friends, loved ones, and ministry tools to guide our life to successfully stay on the path the Lord has anointed us to walk.

The Holy Spirit blesses us with the fruits of the spirit in _Gal 5:22-25_, Supernatural divine Love, Joy, Peace, Patience, Gentleness, Kindness, Faithfulness, Goodness and Spiritual Self-Control. It is easy to maintain these attributes when things are going great in our life. However, these gifts are given to us by the Holy Spirit to truly anoint us whenever we are in a crisis: to be overcomers and gain victory over the natures of the flesh; that Satan uses to bring hatred, anger, vengeance, jealousy, envy, greed, gossip, insecurities, and skepticism, bearing false witness against others. Thus, these end up ruling in making your choices to get through the crisis. Satan wants us to be destroyed through the crisis at hand. If we agree with Satan's natures of the flesh, Satan wins. We are supposed to give it all to Christ.

Phil 1:21 God tells us to "die to the natures of the flesh is to gain in Christ." Yes, we gain in having a forgiving heart, _Luke 23:34_ "Forgive them for they know not what they do" We gain in _2nd Peter 1:3,11,_ "seeing that His divine power has granted us everything pertaining to life and Godliness, through the true knowledge of HIM who called us by HIS own glory and excellence." _John 12:44-46_ God gave the energy of the Holy Spirit empowerment to send Christ into the world. "Whoever believes in me, believes not only in me but believes in the one who sent me. And he who sees Me sees Him who sent Me. I have come into the world as a light, so that no one who believes in Me should ever stay in darkness."

1st John 1:7-9 "walk in the light as Christ walks in the light." _Matt 5:14,16_ "you are the light of the world." Through Christ going to the father to send the spirit of truth; the holy spirit energy so as we will not stay in darkness but excel to the Glory of God. We are created in God's Image. "In the same way, let your light shine before others, that they may see your good deeds and glorify your Father in heaven."

When I was in Israel with Diana Jarrett in 1983, we had a small group of people. As I remember maybe only 9. We were traveling to all the places where Christ had walked. There was surely a powerful radiance and an anointing upon our group. My Prayer language was in auto pilot wherever we went. Truly" praying over everything never ceasing:" _1st Thes. 5:16_ . The first and only time I lived for days praying nonstop. The Glory of God was evident .. Leaving Israel and going to Rome strangers would come up to me saying " I see light sparks shooting out of your eyes." A friend arranged for me to join him and group of young ladies from His Modeling agency at the disco night club "Jackie O's". These girls kept staring at me in wonderment then one by one they couldn't stop asking, "How do you get your eyes to have shooting stars coming out of them? I see light sparks!"

I shared how, "I have just spent days in prayer asking God to anoint me in the Holy Spirit. When we do not let the cares of the world consume us and just give the Lord our full-time love, praise, and worship, He anoints us in different ways. This has not happened to me before, but I have seen these light sparks in four other people in my life, so I am sure it won't last forever but I do not know how or why it is happening to me now. I feel the Holy Spirit in me is very powerful right now. Loving Jesus gives us a Holy Spirit anointing and that can manifest a radiance in different ways at different times." They listened intently!

Sharing this story reminds me of the 3rd time I went to the heavenlies, I had been on several TV shows, Bob Hope, Laugh-IN, Joey Bishop, and Johnny Carson. I was invited to go to Acapulco, Mexico October 1969 with a group from England; Laugh-In, Jeremy Loyd, Joan Collins joined the group also, all of us, were staying at Leslie Bricusse's hacienda. We went out night clubbing at Armando's Le Club dancing and meeting up with friends, and also, Waren Avis, my aunt MaryJane knew him and his sister. I was invited to come back to Acapulco, by Buck Rodgers on January 1st 1970 for all the jet set big and fabulous season parties..

This is when I met Jack Jones for the 1st time. Oh, so many people I was meeting living life in the fast lane. Daytime lunching at the Villa Vera, chatting with Frank Sinatra and Kirk Kerkorian, who remarked how they liked my ½ page color Photo in the Mexican newspaper. A few days later I joined a group from Brazil, Roberto had a 100' all teak three mast sailing yacht. We sailed to Pichilingue Bay where the President of Mexico had his beach house. What a beautiful day; we took the speedboat down from the yacht to go to the beach for a picnic.

I had lost that inner peace I had all my life. So many exciting things were happening, yet I felt so very dead inside. Becoming numb to "The F word" as it was coming out of my mouth. I walked far away from my friends on the beach. Desperately, crying out to the Lord, "Jesus have I been so rotten that I have lost you forever, have I lost you forever, Lord please give me a sign that I know that I haven't lost you forever!" Nonstop tears ran down my face, yet my eyesight became pristine. I could count each grain of sand as I fell straight like an ironing board, face forward into the sand. My spirit left my body, I knew this had happened to me twice before, so I was not afraid. Plus, I was a mature adult now not the child I was before, so my understanding was greater, and my awareness was keen. Whatsoever, I focused on became a highly spiritual experience, I could see the photosynthesis, of the sun's energy going into the plants making oxygen from carbon dioxide. Everything was enhanced in a supernatural beauty! Yet, I felt more like me than ever before, I knew who I was and could feel it so strongly, with a divine perpetual Love, Joy, Peace, Comfort, and this empowerment filling me up. I knew who I was as a shining light of God Almighty, pure and anointed.

I could see and hear my friends, as they ran towards my body laying straight flat face downward in the sand. They were screaming out in a panic, "Linda, Linda are you Ok?", another saying, "Is she dead? She is not moving. Linda, answer us!"

I did not want to return into that body in the sand, I wanted to stay in the beauty of God's glory in me and around me. I was in the most amazing place full of God's grace, a supernatural pure divine love that cannot be described here in earthly body. The omnibenevolence in the character of The Trinity is the most powerful brilliance.

I had asked the question and now God was answering me, I felt precious unto the Lord. He said, "You have received me, I AM, your salvation, Go and walk in my Spirit and live by my word. You have eternal Life."

I said, "No! Lord, Please I want to stay here!"

Three times I argued with the Lord, He repeated back to me what he said, "Walk in my spirit, Live by my word. You have eternal life. You have work to do for me on earth!" As my girlfriend finally got to me, I could see her hand reaching toward my shoulder to turn me over, Sap I returned into my body and before she could touch me, I started to try and get up. They were all screaming in unison, "Linda, what happened? are you ok?"

As I tried to move my arms to push myself up, I felt as if they were springs going back into the earth and a force was springing me toward heaven again. The sensation was powerful and remarkable, three times this actually stopped me from standing up. Then the same feeling came over my legs, as if I was springing up and down. As I attempted to answer my friends as sand was stuck in my mouth, I guess I went down with a smile on my face. All I could say to them was, "I am fine, I am fine" spiting sand out of my mouth, the Lord spoke to me telling me to, "Go into the water now." I thought, 'I can hardly stand up, let alone walk to the water.' Again, three times God told me to go into the water. Finally, I gained strength and coordination to hobble to the water. As the waves came over me, I felt as if the water was going right through me, a pure cleansing of my sins. When I came out of the water, I just told my friends, "I am fine, I'm ok. don't worry." But I did not feel compelled to share my experience with them. It was mine to cherish… thought provoking to say the least.

They all agreed, it was time to go back to the yacht, so we all boarded the speedboat. Now on the yacht, I stayed very quiet on the trip back to Acapulco Bay. I reflected about my life and what I had been doing, not going to church and using the "F" word. Then remembering when I was about twelve years old, I was riding my horse, April, a beautiful Tennessee walking filly, up in the front paddock by the roadside of our property. A truck of inmates drove by screaming a word I had never heard before. (the "F" word) My heart felt pierced, and a defiling feeling rushed through my body. Riding, April, fast back up to the house tears rolled down my face. My Mother alarmed said, "What happened?" I told her what the men in the truck screamed at me.. she told me, "That is a very bad word don't you ever say that again." I felt like some kind of evil just pierced my spirit and it was very painful! Later in my life, I found out the acronym *Fornication Under Command of the King.*

Back in the 1700's when England ruled over Scotland and Ireland and if the English landowner fancied a young maiden: he would go to the king and get a writ that allowed him to rape the maiden before her vows were made the day of her wedding. She and the groom could not protest, or they would be killed and if a baby was born 9 months later, no one knew if the baby was from the rape or her husband consoling her after the rape. This " F" word defiles man, woman and child. *Proverbs 18:21* Words create life or death. Remember *the words you speak might make these things you speak about actually happen.*

But when we become desensitized to vulgar words because everyone is using the "F" word as every other word out of their mouths, it can easily become a lifestyle. I asked the Lord, "forgive me for using that word and forgive me for whatever else I have done, I am so sorry Lord". Once I asked for forgiveness is when I felt an extra degree of pure joy and peace enter me.

After that day everywhere I went people were coming up to me saying, "I have seen you in several places and you have a radiance, a happiness that just is coming out of you. Who are you?"

Or hippies would come up to me saying, "I want what you're on! What are you taking?" My replies would vary depending on who was asking but I would talk about Jesus giving us the Holy Spirit and we need to fellowship, worship, and praise the Lord. We are the light of the Lord. I didn't know my scriptures back then so I could not give them God's word to validate why this was happening to me. It was like I was walking in a bubble of light that truly effected people's hearts.

Chapter 10 The Lord's Prayer in Depth
Matt. 6: 9-13

Our Father who art in heaven, _Exodus 21: 2,3._ **"I am the Lord your God, you shall have no other gods before me."**

Hallowed be thy name _Exodus 21:7._ **"You shall not take the name of the Lord your God in vain."**

Thy Kingdom Come, _2nd Peter 1:3 &11_ **"seeing that HIS divine power has granted us everything pertaining to life and Godliness, through the true knowledge of HIM who called us by HIS own glory and excellence. - For in this way the entrance into the eternal kingdom of the LORD and SAVIOR JESUS CHRIST, will be abundantly supplied to you." _2nd Peter 3:13"_ according to HIS promise we are looking for a new heaven and a new earth, in which righteousness dwells."**

Thy will be done. _1st. John 1: 7-9._ **"It is God's will that we walk in the light as He himself is in the light, we have fellowship with one another and the blood of Jesus, HIS son, cleanses us from all sin. If we confess to Jesus our sins, He is faithful and righteous to forgive us our sins and to cleanse us from all unrighteousness."**

1st John 1: 15-17. **"Do not love the world, nor the things of the world. If anyone loves the world, the love of the Father is not in him. For all that is in the world, the lust of the flesh, the lust of the eyes, and the boastful pride of life, is not from the Father, but from the world and the world is passing away and, also, its lust but the one who does the will of God abides forever". Now place your confidence in Christ and in the ways of God learning the ways of the Holy Spirit.**

{This wisdom comes through fellowship, worship and praise which truly guides us to the will of God through truth. We gain pure, and true divine wisdom. _Romans 10:17_ faith comes by hearing and hearing the word of God}

(Look up these scriptures. _Eph. 6:10-19,_ Apply the Holy Armor of God. _Gal.5: 22-25,_ The fruits of the Spirit. _1st Cor. 12: 4- 12,_ The gifts of the spirit...)

Eph.5:2-21 **"Walk in love, just as Christ also loved you and gave himself up for us... do not let immortality or any impurity or greed continue to be named among you. You have been forgiven, do not go back to your old ways." (Remember whenever you swear evil words, and _Damn_ anything in life, you give Satan power to make your circumstances worse. (_Do not use the "F" word, Acronym: **F**ornication **U**nder **C**ommand of the **K**ing]. This is not a casual slang word. Words have power for what they are intended. The "F" word defiles woman, man, and family. Back when England ruled over Scotland and Ireland; if the landowner fancied a young maiden, he would go to the King and get a writ to rape the maiden the day of her wedding before her vows were made. She and the groom could not protest, or they would be killed. And, if a child was born nine months later, no one knew if that child came from the rape or the husband consoling her. There is no consent to being raped._ Watch the movie _Braveheart._) Oxford dictionary at one point had consent instead of command by the King. " No woman gives consent to be raped.**

Eph.5:10-21, **"There must be no filthiness, silly talk or coarse jesting amongst you but rather give thanks for all things...... You have an inheritance in the kingdom of Christ and God Almighty. For** the fruit of the Spirit of light consist in all goodness, righteousness, and truth. Trying to learn what is pleasing to the Lord... So then do not be foolish but understand what the will of the Lord is: Do not get drunk with wine for that is dissipation but be filled with the Holy Spirit; Speaking to one another in Psalms, Hymns, and spiritual songs, singing and making melody with your heart to the Lord. Always giving thanks for all things in the name of The Lord JESUS CHRIST to GOD, even the FATHER." (Praise, worship and fellowship creates energy and you will receive divine wisdom)

On earth as it is in heaven, *1st Cor. 15:21,* "For since by man, in Adam, came death for all man. So also, by man, in Christ in HIS Holiness, came the resurrection of the dead that all shall be made alive who believe in Christ, The Lord as Savior." *John 6:51.* "I Am the living bread who came down out of heaven; if anyone eats of this bread, they will live forever." *Matt.16:19..* "I will give you the keys of the kingdom of heaven; and whatever you shall bind on earth shall be bound in heaven, and whatever you shall loose from Heaven shall be loosen on earth." *Isaiah 55:11..* "So shall My Word go forth and not return void unto me but shall accomplish all that I desire it to achieve. For you will go out with joy and be led forth with peace."

Give us this day our daily bread *John 6:35, 53-56.* "I AM the bread of life; he who comes to me shall not hunger, and who believes in ME shall never thirst. He who eats this bread of life as my flesh and drinks this wine as my blood has eternal life, and I will raise him up." (It is important to hold onto these truths with every communion you take. This takes the control of the flesh away from our bodies and restores our bodies to become the Temple of the Holy Spirit; with a renewed power in the anointing of Christ authority in us, His Saints.)

1st Cor. 11:24,25. Jesus took the bread, gave thanks and broke it saying, " This is my body, which is for you: do this in remembrance of Me." (the broken body of Christ broke all the bad consequences of all Sin in our bodies and restored us to the righteousness of God.)

Jesus took the wine saying, "This cup is the new covenant in my blood: do this in remembrance of Me." (Christ blood empowers us with God Almighty's abundant blessings and allows the HOLY SPIRIT anointing to enter us, HIS Saints in Christ, being renewed by God's grace and mercy. Just, as the fruit from the tree of the knowledge of good and evil took away our pure righteousness, divine wisdom and true fellowship with God Almighty with one bite: we were transformed into flesh being creatures. Which also allowed Satan to fuel our desires, to satisfy the lust in the natures of the flesh. "The knowledge of good and evil", makes us feel good about doing bad things because the lust desires of the flesh are being satisfied.

So as this anointed communion breaking of the bread and new covenant wine transforms us into *Christlike beings,* gaining back divine wisdom and real power from God Almighty, conquering the evil lust natures of the flesh and Christ stops the curse of death in Hell for all who ask forgiveness for their sins)

Phil. 4:19 "The Lord God will supply all our needs according to HIS Riches in glory in Jesus Christ and those are vast and bountiful." (We are *blessed, Spiritually, Physically, Mentally, Emotionally, Chemically, Electrically, And Financially...*)

Forgive us our trespasses as we forgive those who trespass against us, _Romans 12:14,_ "Bless those who persecute you; bless and curse not." _1st Peter 3:9_ "Not returning evil for evil, or insult for insult, but giving a blessing instead; for you were called for the very purpose that you might inherit a blessing." _Eph. 4:32 ,_ "Be kind to one another, tender-hearted, forgiving each other, just as God in Christ has also forgiven you." (God forgives us with tremendous Love and abundant Joy forgetting the trespass completely. God shows us by example; how he wants us to forgive, so as we inherit that blessing of HIS pure LOVE.) _Matt 6:14,15_ If you do not forgive then God will not forgive you and you will live in the consequences of your unforgiveness. _Matt. 7:1-3_ For with what judgement you judge, you shall be judged: and what measure you condemn, it shall be measured unto you also.

Yet, God wants you to forgive with a loving heart so that Christ can change the bad consequence into a blessing because you have forgiven others of their trespasses'. So do not gossip to others about how someone hurt you. We are called to pray for them so as Satan can no longer fuel their weaknesses. Amen.

**Take us out of Temptation and Deliver Us from Evil: _James 1:13,14._ "Let no man say, when he is tempted, I am tempted by God; For God cannot be tempted by evil, and he himself does not tempt anyone. Each one is tempted when he is carried away by his own lust". (God does not cause or lead us into evil temptations to learn anything in life.) _1st. Cor. 10:13._ "No temptation has overtaken you that is not common to man, now know this that God is faithful and will provide the way of Escape." _2nd Peter 2:9._ "The Lord knows how to rescue The Godly from temptation." Those who are unrighteous have not recognized their sin and have not asked for forgiveness. (God set into motion the laws of consequence upon creation. He does not do bad things to us: It is our choices that do that! If we make wrong choices we get bad consequences; If we make right choices we get good consequences; If we make Godly choices we get great consequences!)

Only Jesus Christ, the Savior of mankind, can make a good change within the course of all consequences. God Almighty took a part of himself to create the word: The word of creation is the Son of God, Jesus Christ, who came down to earth dwelling among mankind to show us the way, the truth, the light of life. We are recreated by the word of creation. So, as we could gain back our authority in being created in God's image: full of God's power giving us many blessings through the empowerment of the Holy Spirit anointing.

John 14:12-30. We gain the authority to conquer the evil natures of the flesh that Satan birthed into mankind through Adam's disobedience.)

Gal. 1:3,4." Grace to you and peace from God the Father and the Lord Jesus Christ, who gave himself for our sins, that he might Deliver us out of this present evil age, according to the will of God the Father to whom the glory be forever."

For thine is the kingdom, the power and the glory forever.... _1st Chron. 29:11-13._ "Thine, O Lord, is the Greatness, the Power, the Glory, the Victory and the Majesty, indeed everything that is in the heavens and the Earth; thine is the Dominion, both riches and pure honor come from thee and dost rule overall. In the hand lies the power and might to make great and to strengthen everyone. Therefore, THE LORD GOD ALMIGHTY, we thank thee and praise thy glorious name forevermore. Amen"

By LindaJane Chapman via a Holy Spirit anointing

Chapter 11 Gain Faith to Change Harmful Weather

We are made to be creative in the image of God. God gave us so much power when he formed man in the garden of the Eden. *Genesis 1:3* God spoke let there be light and there was light. *John 1:1-3.* The word of creation in the beginning was God and was with God and all things were created through him, the word of creation, Christ the son of God our redeemer.

Satan used idolatry to bamboozle Adam out of his birthright. *Genesis 3:5* By first saying " you will be like God knowing good and evil."

Matthew 17:20 Christ said, "if you have faith like a grain of mustard seed, you will say to this mountain, 'move from here to there', and it will move, and nothing will be impossible.

The energy from the Trinity with faith enables us, who are renewed in Christ redemption salvation to have tremendous authority here on earth: if we use God's word. *Proverbs 3:5,6* Trust in the Trinity with all your heart, and do not allow your natures of the flesh to hinder your power.

All energy forces in the universe and on the earth's, surface are created by God. Satan takes the little-known substance and gives it to science to pervert the energy. Satan can do nothing without a human being facilitating Satan's vile ideas. The natures of the flesh are birth into mankind by Satan seducing Adam into idolatry. The forces of energy that science knows works in many levels in which mankind has utilized the knowledge they have. Ahhhh, yet science has only been able to use what they have learned, and those things can bring many side effects. Because they don't know what the unknown ingredients are that God Almighty has Placed into anything and everything that counters the side effects in the little facts that science knows. The word of creation has more power to alter whatever man-made science has developed. If we choose to utilize the power God has given us.

Mark 11:23, for assuredly, , I say to you, whoever says to this mountain, 'be removed and be cast into the sea', and does not doubt in his heart, but believes that those things he says will be done, he will have whatever he says.

Eph 6:19 pray also for me and whenever I speak, that the words may be given to me so that I will be bold to make known the mystery of the gospel. Galatians 6:7 , Romans 6:23 , Proverbs 18:20 – 21 you will have to live with the consequences of everything you say. What you say can preserve life or destroy it; so, you must accept the consequences of your words.

We must be wise not saying things that are harmful to human beings. God made the laws of consequence upon creation. If you make wrong choices, you get bad consequence, make right choices, you good consequence but if you make godly choices, you get great consequence: only Christ can change a bad consequence to a good or great consequence depending upon how we asked for forgiveness or for his help.

Luke 1:37 nothing is impossible with God. Trust in God. don't doubt.

Psalms 32:8 God instructs, teaches, and guides us daily in all our endeavors.

Psalms 62:5 – 8. My soul, waits only upon God; for my expectation is from God. God only is my rock and my salvation; he is my defense I shall not be moved. God is the rock of my strength. My refuge is in God. Trust in God at all times; ye people, pour out your heart unto God. God is a refuge for us a solid rock.

I pray these Scripture to stop all earthquakes from harming my property. God is my rock I shall not be moved.

We never know when an earthquake could happen, but I know my house will stand.

Joshua 24:15 as for me and my house, we will serve the Lord.

Exodus 12:13 we stand with the blood of the Lamb and all evil must pass over and never harm us. Amen

When I was a child there was a tornado coming towards our house. My mother screaming," Linda get in the cellar now!!" But my legs were frozen pipes in the ground. I didn't learn what I did that day from going to the Methodist Church. God told me to reach out my hand, point my finger at the tornado and out of my mouth came these words" you tornado will not harm our property; turn, you will turn in the name of Jesus" our house is on the highest hill in that area and that tornado was coming right at our house 15 acres back from the roadway. When it was all over, we all came out of the cellar; we checked on our neighbor across the street. And they had one shingle that flew off the garage. But with that I knew that tornado turned. Trust in the Lord be obedient to what he tells you to say, and it shall be your outcome.

The word of God's power is here now on earth. We must have faith and believe. *Romans 10:17* Faith comes by hearing and hearing the word of God.

A few years later a big fire blowing through the countryside. The strong winds were coming toward our property. My mother called my dad, he said, " get all the paddock gates locked, so the horse don't get blocked up there. Open up the stalls and let the horses out the main gate; we'll get them later!'

I ran to the stables did as he said. But then I stood there looking at the raging fire as the wind hit my face. Once again, the Lord stopped me in my tracks. God said, "reach out your hand and point your finger at that fire and tell the winds to turn." I did that and I said, "fire you will not harm our property, fire you will not touch a blade of our grass or our trees: Lord make the wind change now." I felt the wind leave my face and go to the side of my head as I watched the fire change directions, The horses were running wild, and my mother stopped the car on our winding driveway picking me up as we fled our property. Later when we returned, we could see how the fire burned all the way to the lake not touching our property or harming any buildings on the neighbor's property.

This is a prayer to dismantle all storms in life. Agreement between believers is paramount to conquer all negative forces in the atmosphere.

So, when something is rising up against our land, our homes, our belongings, our animals, and our family, it is important to share this prayer. *Isaiah 41:13* the Lord God Almighty says fear not for I will hold your right hand and help you.

John 14:12 – 31 Jesus told us he was going to the father to send the spirit of truth, the Holy Spirit, to give us an advocate of authority.

We are believing in Christ and have a Holy Spirit energy empowerment over all things: we can command the angels and saints to assist us to dismantle the power in any earthquake, tsunami, hurricane, typhoon ,cyclone, tornado, thunderstorm and lightning. We asked the Lord to cross an interference to dismantle these earthly things of harm that they peter out and go into nothingness. No matter what the chemical and/or electrical or laser forces used it cannot be utilized by any energy force to go anywhere but to stop in its trail, shutting down completely. *Mark 4:39* Jesus got up and rebuked the wind and told the waves be still and He said unto the sea Peace be still. And the wind ceased, and there was a great calm..

The word of God alone can make the wind and water obey. *Psalms 23:4 yea, though I walk through the valley of the shadow of death, I will fear no evil; for thou art with me, thy rod and thy staff they comfort me.*

In Jesus name we have authority. Jesus showed us how to calm the storm. So can we calm the storm: as God Almighty gives us his word and his word is the energy of creation above all other forces in the universe.

Isaiah 55:11 God's word will not return void unto him but will accomplish all that is purpose to achieve we will go out with joy and be led forth with peace amen.

God's word is omniscient, omnipotent, and omnipresent his power is in his word when we use it, we have victory. *Psalms 115:3, Isaiah 55:11 Jeremiah 32:17 Genesis 18:14 Psalms 105:24 – 25 Genesis 45:5 –8 Romans 9:18 acts2: 23 , 4:28; Deuteronomy 18:21 – 22 Titus 1:2 Numbers 23:19 Matthew 6:26 – 30, Matthew 10:29 – 30 Proverbs 16:33; acts 17, Isaiah 44:28, Psalms 33:10 – 11,   acts 2:23 – 24,*

Psalms 139:13 – 16, Romans 11:33 – 36 , James 7:13 – 17, Ephesians 2:8 – 10, acts 13:48, Exodus 6:7 John 6: 44, 65 , Philippians 1:29, lam 3:37-38 , Romans 8:28, Ephesians 1:11, Psalms 147:5, John 21:17, Hebrews 4:12 – 13, 1st John 3:20, 1ˢᵗ Samuel 10, Kings 13:1 – 4 2ⁿᵈ Kings 8:12 , Psalms 139:4 , acts 2:23 , acts 4:27 – 28 , Genesis 18:20 – 21 , John 14:6, Genesis 26:3, Exodus 6:7, 2ⁿᵈ Corinthians 6:16, Genesis 17:7, lev 26:12, jer 7:23, 11:4 Ezek 11:20 , 14:11 , 36:28 , 37:27 , heb 11:16 , rev 21:3, ; Isaiah 7:14, Matthew 1:23, John 1:14, rev 1:7

These are the Scriptures that validate the Omni powers of the Trinity. We are created in God's image renewed through Christ's salvation.

We as Christ vessels command the heavenly Holy forces to go forth and dismantle any and all storms that come near us or our family and loved ones.. By the power of creation which is more powerful than all synthetic substances...

We praise the Lord and rejoice in victory. Trust in the Trinity only all inclusively and speak God's word boldly.

Matthew 8:13 go and as you believe it will it be done. We are created in God's image to utilize the energy forces of creation.

Psalms 118:24 this is the day that the Lord has made we will rejoice and be glad in it. *Romans 8:28* all things work together for good for those who love the Lord and are called according to his purpose. 1ˢᵗ *Thessalonians 5:16* pray over everything never ceasing. Lord be with me in this that I do. I trust in you Lord and your Trinity. Amen Praise the Lord,

By LindaJane Chapman via a Holy Spirit anointing

Chapter 12 "The Prayer of the Morning"

John 1:1-3 " in the beginning was the word, and the Word was with God, and the Word was God. Christ was in the beginning with God and all things were created through him. The word of the creation is Christ, the Son of God." We are re-created in Christ to be renewed in God's image. We own our identity in Christ, we are made in the image of God to be the temple of the Holy Spirit. "In God We Trust" In "The Trinity" is our power here on earth.

Lord whenever we make choices from our flesh, we place ourselves in Satan's battleground and You, The Trinity can come there and help us battle the forces of evil. However, whenever we make choices from the Spirit of Truth, we are in The Trinity's playground and Satan can not come there. Lord, you place that Holy Hedge *Job 1:8* around us to stop Satan.

I champion each person to daily pray scriptures; this gives us through Christ a supernatural divine wisdom, true fellowship, anointed worship, pure righteousness, and a real refined understanding of the amazing empowerment we gain from the energy in The Holy Spirit authority on earth.

Matt 18:20 We pray these scriptures together for ourselves, all our family, friends, and loved ones to abundantly bless our lives as "Lord, you are with us where two or more are gathered." *Job 1:8* We pray the Lords Holy hedge around us all, even unto our enemies to stop Satan from fueling vile wicked ideas into all of us. (From being offended, having anger, hatred, vengeance, gossip to intentionally hurting others and disrespect for what another person has gone through. When being under the attack from the wicked forces in the universe people are making wrong choices through the natures of the flesh moving in their emotions.) God places a Holy Hedge around us all when we activate it. The same hedge he placed around Job; that he gained the true and pure blessings in abundance from God Almighty is also our Holy Hedge when we use it. Agreeing with Satan's ideas takes that protective hedge away.

Proverbs 18:21 "Death and life are in the power of the tongue" Lord give us the wisdom to build life and bring healing in all our endeavors daily. *Matt. 7:1-2* "Do Not Judge, or you too will be judged. For in the same way, you judge others, you will be judged, and with the same measure you use, it will be measured to you." Lord Help us all to pray for each other *Luke 23:34* "forgive them for they know not what they do." Lord, you know it is the natures of the flesh that Satan fuels to make people do offensive things against themselves and others.

Eph. 6:10-13 "**finally, my brethren be strong in the Lord and the power in his might. We put on the whole armor Lord that we may be able to stand against the wiles of the devil. For we wrestle not against flesh and blood but against principalities, powers, rulers of the darkness of this world and spiritual wickedness in high places**" However, we are the victors because we are the temple of The Holy Spirit.

Matt. 6: 9-13 **"Lord, take us out of evil." I know Lord, you would never lead us into evil because your word tells us that you would not.** *James 1:13-16* "*let no man say when he is tempted, I am tempted by God; for God cannot be tempted with evil neither does he tempt any man with evil, **but every man is tempted, when he is drawn away by his own lust.**"*

1st Cor. 10:13 **"no temptation is overtaking you that is not common to man and God will make a way of escape."** *2nd Peter 2:9* The Lord knows how to rescue the godly from trials and to hold the unrighteous accountable on the day of judgement. Ahh, the laws of consequences can only be changed through asking Christ for forgiveness. "The Lord forgives me for my flesh choices that took me out of my spiritual connection with him, which helps me make better choices when the Holy Spirit leads me in truth and wisdom."

Fallen angels work through man via the natures of the flesh, psychics, mediums, astrologers, stay away from them *Colossians 2:8* **"see to it that no one takes you captive by philosophy, and empty deceit, <u>according to human traditions</u>, according to elemental demons and evil spirits of the world, yoga, karma, and** *not according to Christ empowerment in the Holy Spirit of divine truth."* **We thank you Jesus for your strength and divine wisdom given to us, to know the difference and not be fooled.**

Eph.6:14. **"We stand therefore, having belted our loins with truth."** Lord, it is your word that enlightens us with divine truth. *1st.Cor.12:4-12* "Revelation, prophecy, wisdom, discernment, casting out evil, prayer language, interpretation of prayer language, healing, and effecting of miracles."

These are the gifts of the spirit that Christ uses to enhance our knowledge in the spiritual realm. Lord, we want to use these gifts for ourselves and for ministering to others in whatever the challenge is at that moment in time. We are your vessels here on earth. Lord, make us proficient in these gifts. *Mark 17:16.* **" in my name, (Jesus said) , you will cast out demons and they will flee."**

John 14:12-28. "Very truly I tell you, whoever believes in me will do the works, I have been doing, and they will do even greater things than these, because I AM going to the Father. And I will do whatever you ask in my name... I will ask the Father to send the Spirit of Truth 'the Holy Spirit' to be with you as an advocate forever."

Proverbs 18:10. "The name of the Lord is a strong fortress; the Godly will run to him and are safe."

Ephesians 6:14. "the breastplate of righteousness." We are transformed from darkness to light. We cast out the vile natures of the flesh in *Galatians 5:19- 21,* 26 "ego, envy, greed, pride; worry, fear, guilt; gossip, contrariness, orneriness, stubbornness; criticism, skepticism, negativity; procrastination, irresponsibility, impatience, distraction; vengeance, jealousy, covetousness, stealing, hatred, anger, murder; drunkenness, carousing, adultery; idolatry, sorcery, philosophies of the world; judgmental attitude, condemnation, self-centeredness, self-righteousness, self-destruction, generational curses; illness, injury illness, bio-chemical illness, all disease, and all sexual perversions must flee from us all." We Pray our family, and our loved ones to learn these truths. *Isaiah 54: 17* "for no weapon formed against us will ever prosper!"

Christ, reveals, to us his saints, that if we in _Phil 1:21_, 'die to the natures of the flesh than we gain in Christ anointing:' supernatural divine wisdom, true fellowship, anointed worship, pure righteousness, and a real energy empowerment of the Holy Spirit. This is what we strive for Lord! To know you are living through us and by your word we excel.

Ephesians 6:15 "our feet are shod in the preparation of the gospel of peace." Holy Spirit please guide us whenever we speak that we will find favor in all our endeavors. Lord, you give us the spirit of truth.

We choose to embrace these fruits of the spirit: divine peace and pure truth from heaven and do not distinguish them by the ways of the world. We have real power in Christ word. Forgiveness is paramount. _Matt.6:14,15_ "If you do not forgive others of their sins, your Father in heaven will not forgive your sins." You make yourself live through the consequence. God wants you to forgive others.

This does not mean you lose your salvation: it means that the consequence for your sin cannot be changed by Christ renewal. Only as you forgive then Christ can change the consequences of the sin.

Galatians 5: 22-25 , "empower us Lord with your divine supernatural love, joy, peace, patience, gentleness, kindness, faithfulness, goodness and spiritual self-control". We must agree to have the Holy Spirit to lead us.

1st Corinthians13:4-13 "the greatest of these is love: God's Omnibenevolence."

Ephesians 6: 16 "above all taking the shield of faith where with we will be able to extinguish all the fiery darts of the wicked". We are in a spiritual war daily, so we want to use the tools you have given us Lord.

Isaiah 41:13 "for I, thy God will hold your right hand, saying unto you, fear not I will help you, amen"

Matthew 16:23, **When** evil attacks us or our loved ones. Remember what Christ said to Peter "get behind me, Satan you are stumbling block to me. Your concerns are not of God, but you merely think of human concerns." If we choose, we can be spiritual beings 1st and foremost.

Lord, please stop us from making choices or decisions from our emotions. We want to make Godly choices. (Lord, upon creation you made the laws of consequence. If we make wrong choices, we get bad consequences, if we make right choices, we get good consequences, but if we make Godly choices, we get great consequences.) Father God Almighty we Praise You and Thank You for Christ's redemption salvation that conquers the natures of the flesh and broke the curse of death that Satan birthed into mankind through Adam's disobedience. We Love you, Lord, for your salvation gives us back the authority to live in a supernatural divine fellowship with you in the Trinity. Only you Lord Jesus can change a bad consequence to a good or great consequence, depending upon how we ask for forgiveness or for your help.

Roman 7: 19,20 "for I do not do the good I want, but the evil I do not want is what I keep doing. Now if I do that which I should not. It is no longer I that do it, but the sin that dwells within me" You can cast that nature out by Christ Holy Spirit authority over sin!

Romans 6:17 "a Christian can still sin by a freewill choice in your nature's of the flesh but is no longer helpless slave to sin". _1st Cor. 3:16._ "do you not know that God's Spirit dwells in you." This power in Christ conquers the vile Natures of the flesh which tries to defeat our Holy Spirit power in Christ anointing authority in us. We only have victory when we recognize and defeat the natures of the flesh.

Isaiah 55:11, **"Lord God Almighty, your words will not return void to you, but will accomplish all that is purposed to achieve. We will go out with joy and be led forth with peace".**

John 20: 21-22 "My peace be with you ! As the father has sent me, I'm sending you, receive the Holy Spirit." Lord, you have empowered us, who have received your salvation with the same power that God sent you to earth with and that you ascended with into heaven.

John 14: 16-30. "I will ask the father and he will give you the Spirit of truth. The people of the world cannot accept him or know him, but you know him; he lives in you, for you are the temple of the Holy Spirit."

Thank you, Christ for re-creating us in God's image. Lord we want to align ourselves with _Philippians 4:8._ "so, we want to dwell on whatsoever things are true, just, honest, pure, lovely, and of a good report (the A+ for what we need to happen in our life) where there is virtue and justice". We want to be anointed by the empowerment of the Holy Spirit guiding us. We all are truly blessed with _Phil 4:13._ "we can do all things through Christ who strengthens us." _Phil 4 :19._ "God will supply our every need spiritually, physically, emotionally, mentally, chemically, electrically, and financially."

Matthew 17: 20-21. "The Lord gives us that small mustard seed that grows fast into a 30-foot-tall mighty tree of faith." That seed Lord, you gifted each person with upon our creation; we want this power to hear your truth; so, as we grow fast in faith.

Teach us Lord to hear your voice, we desire to recognize our obedience within your guidance. _Psalm 32:8._ "Lord you instruct, teach, and guide us in all our endeavors."

Matthew 6:9-13 "On earth as it is in heaven." We have the power to bring heaven to earth. Teach us how to exercise your divine power, Lord.

Matthew 8:5-13, Lord, we want to grow in faith just as the centurion was of strong faith. He said, "Lord you don't have to go to my home. Lord, your word is sufficient! Just say the word and my servant will be healed" Lord, you show us how to believe when you answered the centurion, "go thy way and as you believed, so be it done unto you." _Lord, we worship you Father God, Christ our Savior, and the empowerment of the Holy Spirit energy; (The Trinity). Lord, you give us your_ *powers through your supernatural divine word. Through us using your word we are the vessels empowered by your omnipresent, omnipotent, omniscient, omnibenevolent, authority in the word of creation. Thank you, Jesus, that you enlighten us daily. I love you Jesus.*

Ephesians 6:17 "the helmet of salvation." *John 3:16,* "God so love the world that he gave his only begotten son; that when we believe in Jesus as Lord and ask forgiveness of our sins and we know that only Jesus rose from the dead as our Savior, we are saved." *John 3:17* "God did not send Jesus into the world to condemn the world but that all might be saved through him." *Acts 16:31* "the Lord promised us "if you believe you and your household will be saved." *Genesis 22:2–13* "the Lord will provide a deliverer."

Mark 16:17–18. "Lord, you said that we could pick up any poisonous thing and that it would not harm us in any way". *We thank you Lord for blessing the foods we eat, air we breathe; the water and fluid we drink, all medicine, lotions, cleaning supplies, and paper goods we use. Plus, all machines, cell phones, computer electronics and the energy that makes these work.* We take authority and pray for protection for us, even though we must use these things, Lord, you protect us with your holy armor in *Ephesians 6:10–19* Thank you Lord. You send holy angels to purify everything around and inside us and our loved ones. Jesus, give us restoration over our health and well-being and bring daily healing upon our bodies. amen.

Ephesians 6:17 "Lord we have the sword of the Spirit in our hands which is the word of God". *Romans 10:17* faith comes by hearing and hearing the word of God

Hebrews 4:12 "God's word is alive and active, sharper in a two-edge sword. He divides the soul and the spirit; he judges the thoughts and attitudes of the heart". We seek to have a pure heart, Lord.

Proverbs 3:5, 6 "we lean not unto our own understanding but in all thy ways we acknowledge you Lord that you make straight and direct our paths."

Romans 8:28 "all things work together for good for those who Love the Lord and are called according to his purpose." *1st thes. 5:16-17* God's purpose is that we "pray over everything never ceasing". ' Lord, be with me in this that I do. Guide me, Lord.'

Ephesians 6:18, "praying always with all prayer and supplication in the Spirit and watching their unto with all perseverance and petition for all saints." This scripture establishes we are not angels that we get wings when we die. We are holy saints created in God's image. Angels never get redemption from their disobedience. We praise you Lord for this distinction in your creations.

1st Chronicles 4: 10 "Lord, anoint us all and our loved ones, increase our territories to bless us all. Keep us all from harm so that we will be free from pain." Lord, give us favor among people to be chosen for the project at hand. For our path is enhanced; we are blessed, we are your children, we are givers of the land successful in all the gifts which you bestow upon us. Lord, meet our every need. *Philippians 4:19* we are blessed spiritually, physically, mentally, emotionally, electrically, chemically, and financially. I love you, Jesus.

2nd Peter 3:8. "God has perfect timing: never early, never late, God is never in a hurry, but God is always on time".

1st. John 5:7. "for there are three that bear record in heaven: the Father, Christ the word, and the Holy Spirit: and these three are one Trinity."

Lord, we praise your holy name that we are divine by being created in your image: we have power if we choose to exercise it, to learn to practice applying it in our life. Teach us Lord to always be Christlike in our life.

Psalms 118:24. "this is the day that the Lord has made, and we will rejoice and be glad in it." Not in choices made by the natures of the flesh.

Matthew 19:26 "with man this is impossible but with God all things are possible."

Isaiah 14:24 "I have planned, so shall it be, and yes what I have purposed, so shall it stand!"

2nd Peter 1:3, 11 "seeing that his divine power has granted us everything pertaining to life and Godliness, to the true knowledge of him who called us by his own glory and excellence." Christ omniscience is in his word.

1st John 1: 7,9 "We walk in the light as Christ walks in the light." We desire to be Christ-like.

Matthew 5:14,16 "you are the light of the world, because Christ went to the father and sent the spirit of truth, the Holy Spirit is this beautiful energy so that we will not stay in darkness, but we have the light of the Lord which glorifies God".

We Pray in agreement this whole Prayer to bless and anoint the United States of America to become strong again in Christian Values and integrity. Anyone who comes to destroy America will be defeated. We pray for the Lord God Almighty to give supernational wisdom to those who work to make America the best ever; so that our government is anointed by The Trinity. This is your nation, Lord. We stand with you.

Ephesians 6:19, "Lord I pray for me, that utterance may be given unto me, that I may be bold to make known the mysteries of the gospel." All praise and glory to you Lord Jesus, as we receive you, Lord. For you are the only one Lord, who gives us back life and everlasting divine love is your Omnibenevolence through eternity, amen.

Linda Chapman-Henry PrayerCoachUSA.com HolySpiritOne2@aol.com

Dyan Cannon: A Golden Globe Award winner, Academy Award nominated Actress, Author, Producer, Inspirational Christian Evangelist, "Linda's faith in God is evident in all walks of her life....it's a beautiful thing to behold."

Terry Moore: An Academy Award Nominated Actress, Author, Married Howard Hughes. "Linda's Prayer Book is excellent; it helps people to overcome difficult times and it lifts people up! I love Linda, she is a best friend."

Chrystall Friedemann, producer, actor, comedian "Learning the scriptures in my Mother's book " Be Love" putting scriptures in a specific order gives extra understanding of God's word. This book has really helped me out in many of my life experiences, knowing God's word is very powerful!

Gemma Wenger: Evangelist, Television Host, Producer, "Linda Chapman-Henry engages in a whirlwind of exciting experiences propelled by the power of the Holy Spirit. Wherever she goes, supernatural favor and protection accompany her. Linda is a unique talent placed on earth by God for a very special purpose.

Dr. Lee Benton: Actress, Producer, Author, Evangelist. Victory Road Productions: Lee Benton Ministries Intl. Linda Chapman-Henry is a "Warrior Woman" for the Lord....A true TRAILBLAZER and friend who's a beautiful, brilliant, shining light in Hollywood and across the world. This book is a "Must Read" filled with her exciting life changing experiences, wisdom and uplifting scriptures inspired by the Holy Spirit.

**Scan QR code to watch
Acts of the Apostle Broadcast on
YT/TheMarketplaceNetwork:**

or watch Acts of the Apostle at:

The Cross TV - Bishop Gerald Jones: PrayerCoachUSA.com

Vision TV with Adnan Maqsood

**JITA: Jesus is the Answer KTLA
Bishop Ernest Johnson**

**YT/LindaJane Chapman-Henry
PrayerCoachUSA.com**

By LindaJane Chapman via a Holy Spirit anointing